Impruneta May 2005
to Stefania,
Buon Appetito

Carla Geri Camporesi
Barbara Golini

FROM THE ART OF THE MEDICIS
TO THE TABLES OF TODAY

introduction by
Ilaria Della Monica

translation by
Judith Moser

mᵖ

maria pacini fazzi editore

Prima edizione italiana
© maria pacini fazzi editore, lucca 1999
Per la traduzione in inglese: © Copyright 2001
maria pacini fazzi editore
via dell'angelo custode, 33 - 55100 lucca
tel. 0583.440188 - fax 0583.464656
e.mail: mpf@pacinifazzi.it
sito internet: www.pacinifazzi.it

photos reference from Fototeca Alinari - Florence

on the cover:
Anonymous Flemish Artist, *Two women in the kitchen,* Florence, Pitti Palace (in storage)

ISBN 88-7246-486-2

Introduction

The latter years of the fifteenth century saw the emergence of still life paintings. At this time, and until the end of their dynasty and patronage in the middle of the eighteenth century, the grand dukes and princes of the Medici amassed a whole series of these pictures. The still life paintings included in the art collections of this Florentine family are exemplary in their variety of style, beauty of pictorial quality and sheer

abundance, a circumstantial but rich artistic harvest. There are over 400 paintings, a representative spread from which can be distilled the historical development of the genre of still life during this period. These canvases by Italian and foreign artists were either acquired by agents acting on the spot, or they

were directly commissioned from those artists who even at the time were considered to be masters in this field. They document subjects typical of this kind of art: floral compositions, ornamental bowls of fruit, fishes, kitchen interiors. It is easy to understand how such pictures were able to fire the imagination of the authors of this book.

The vivid colours, the excellent and knowledgeable choice of fruit and the refined atmosphere of certain tables all served to inspire, as we know from contemporary documents, digressions on perfumes and fragrances. A floral composition may not necessarily suggest a culinary topic but appears in this text thanks to the delightful little picture of "Mario de' fiori", a work which belonged to the great Prince Ferdinando, depicting a small glass cruet containing a carnation, a convolvulus and a caper flower. There is a wide choice of other typical subjects. We may think of the limpid tempera pictures painted by Giovanna Garzoni for Ferdinando II, transmitting onto paper the pure and enchanting colours of freshly picked plums and cherries, almonds in their shells, or beans, arranged on plates with a graceful rustic simplicity which hints at the presence of scented seasonal flowers. At the same time, we may contemplate the elegant tables illustrated by Dutch artists. Amongst the best and most beautiful is the one by Willelm van Aelst which belonged to

Giovan Carlo, where the head of a ram, with innards attached, the artichoke and the lemon, all have the splendour of hard stone and the colours of precious textiles.

Contemporary paintings help us to understand the diversity of thought which must lie behind such works. The aim was to extol, on the one hand, the simple banquet offered spontaneously by nature, and on the other hand, the sumptuous trappings of an affluent society, such as that of the Dutch. In fact, it is not by chance that the painting of a kitchen interior which begins the book - among the first of its kind in Florence - actually has its origin in the Northern school.

The background evocation of a setting for the dinner of Emmaus is not, in fact, enough to lessen the sense of plenty conveyed by the ostentatious display of poultry, fishes, meat and food in general. In many cases this also applies to the markets painted by Aertsen or Beuckelaer at the end of the sixteenth century, a reflection of whose work can sometimes be found in certain Lombard pictures. In the Medici art collections and in the paintings interspersed in the present text we again find the kitchen portrayed as the domestic space par excellence: it is a room where various kinds of meats and vegetables are prepared for the table. These are paintings of a relatively late date - the first few decades of the 18th century - and they make use of a generally accepted set of pictorial motifs which was no longer limited to any region but had become international: from Flanders (e.g. Houbraken) to Italy (Valentino, Munari).

The hallmark of this type of painting is that of a simple, almost earthy domesticity: typically we find large vegetable baskets tipped at an angle, their sprawling contents, roots and all, bathed in light, at the edges of which various other comestibles are assembled: oysters, white cabbages, bottles, modest dishes of cardoons, of ham, of cooked eggs in earthenware dishes; accompanied by rustic-looking bread and wine served in straw covered flasks. It is a simple, homely vignette whose edges are tinged by the cheerful glow of a fire: blackened walls and

burnished copper utensils are added to the tableau. We are at a far remove from the clamour and noise of the reception room or the salon: here all is intimate, domestic, warm, aromatic and cosy.

The counterpoint to these pictures - these snug interior depictions of domestic kitchens - consists, in the judgment of the great art patrons of the period, of those grandiose and imposing compositions filled with magnificent displays of fruit, of layers of fish, and so forth; a genre which appears with ever greater frequency from the middle of the 17th century.

A good example of the type is the large still life of fish painted by the neapolitan Giuseppe Recco: an artistic masterpiece of its kind, by one of the painters best known at this period for this sort of composition, not least for the life-like scaly freshness he imparted to the fish, that sparkling just-caught look he managed to give them. It was artists of this calibre who inspired Giuseppe Crespi in his still life of fish composed for the Grand Prince Ferdinand. This work whose companion piece is a brace of game has as its centrepiece a large red scorpion-fish; the classical formality of its style confirms that it is the work of a figure painter.

The works of Bartolomeo Bimbi meanwhile can be said to occupy a place apart. A whole host of fruits and vegetables meets the eye: a veritable inventory of all those grown on the estates of Cosimo III, the most important of the artist's patrons. Set usually against a solemn background - such as an idealized representation of their natural surroundings - we see large cascades of cherries, plums or similar fruits, each bunch delicately distinguished through the variety of shades of colour of their species, by the tactile effects of their skin; while a plethora of different baskets, bowls or other containers overflow with apples and pears, underlining how bounteous and plentiful nature is in her gifts. Next to this opulence we see depicted a number of other fruits remarkable either for their size or their fertility, or for belonging to rare and exotic species: a bunch of sweet dates for example, with a group of palms in the background to denote their provenance from torrid, far-away regions.

Ilaria Della Monica

From the art of the Medicis to the tables of today

Anonymous flemish artist, *Two women in the kitchen,* Florence, Pitti Palace (in storage)

Bistecca alla fiorentina / Florentine style beef steak

2 t-bone beef steaks
salt and pepper to taste

It is not difficult to cook a beef steak, but it needs a very delicate touch. First of all, choose top quality meat, cut at least 3 cm(1.1/2 inches) thick. It should not be beaten or seasoned in advance.

The meat must be cooked on a grill which is placed over red-hot embers of coal or wood. As soon as the steak is lightly seared on one side, it should be turned over, and at this moment only, the side which has been grilled should be seasoned with salt and pepper.

This process must be repeated the moment the steak is turned over.

The meat will be more tender if it is cooked "blue", i.e. very rare.

Serve at once.

Filetto di salmone al cartoccio / Fillet of salmon

800 g (2 pounds) of fresh salmon
2 carrots
2 corgettes
2 leeks
pinch of salt and pepper
2 tablespoons extra virgin olive oil
lemon

Skin the salmon and remove all bones. Separately, dice the vegetables into matchstick-size pieces, and parboil in salted water. When the vegetables are parboiled, stop them cooking by refreshing under cold water. Prepare a parcel, using oven paper or aluminium foil, and put the salmon on this, with the vegetables on top. Add salt and pepper and a drizzle of olive oil. Close up the parcel, and cook it in the oven at 180° C. (350 F.) for 30 minutes. Season with oil, lemon, salt and pepper .

Piccioni in tegame / Pigeons in a pan

4 pigeons
50 g (2 oz) bacon
1 small onion
a few bay leaves
salt and pepper to taste
meat extract for the stock

rice pilaf:
400 g (1 pound) rice
half an onion
2 tablespoons (1 oz) butter
½ litre (2 cups) stock

Clean the pigeons carefully and put a bay leaf inside each one. Brown the pigeons evenly in a saucepan, together with the bacon and the finely chopped onion. Continue cooking over a moderate heat for about half an hour, adding a little stock if necessary. When they have finished cooking, cut the pigeons in half, put them on top of the rice pilaf which has been prepared separately, and moisten them with the cooking juices (from the pan).

To prepare the rice pilaf, gently fry half a finely chopped onion in 25 g (approx 1 oz) of butter. When the onion is reduced, add the rice, stirring quickly so that it takes on the flavour, then add the stock and put it all in the oven in a covered dish for 20 minutes at 200° C. (390 F.). The water should be completely absorbed so that the rice is soft with the grains staying well separated.

Giovanni Domenico Valentino, *Kitchen interior,* Florence, Pitti Palace (in storage)

Arrosto con i porri / Roast veal with leeks

800 g (2 pounds) best end of veal
4 leeks (or 4 fresh onions)
1 litre (4 cups) milk
½ glass (1/3 cup) extra virgin olive oil
1 pinch salt, pepper, nutmeg

Put the olive oil in a heavy saucepan, and brown the meat on all sides. When it is brown, and therefore seared, add the leeks (or the onions), thinly sliced into rounds, then cover the pan and cook over a moderate heat until the leeks are reduced. At this point, add the milk, and season with salt, pepper and a pinch of nutmeg. Continue cooking until the milk has nearly all been absorbed. Take the meat out of the pan and keep it warm on a hot dish, with another plate on top. Pass the sauce through a vegetable mill, and then put it back in the saucepan to thicken for a few minutes. Carve the meat into thin slices and serve it hot with the sauce. Any excess sauce can be used to make a quick leek soup. Dilute with stock, and serve with little squares of toast.

Lesso rifatto / Boiled meat, re-cooked

200 g (½ pound) boiled beef
500 g (1 pound) onions
300 g (⅔ pound) peeled tomatoes
3 tablespoons extra virgin olive oil
salt and pepper to taste

Thinly slice the onions and brown them in a saucepan with 3 tablespoonfuls of oil. As soon as the onions are soft, add the tomatoes and season with salt and pepper. Cook the sauce for 10 minutes over a moderate heat. Cut the meat into fair-sized pieces, and add these to the sauce. Cover, and continue cooking for 15 minutes, stirring frequently.
Serve with potatoes (cooked in a light sauce).

Peposo alla fornacina / Brickyard pepper dish

2 kg (4 pounds) muscle of veal
700 g (2 pounds) peeled tomatoes
10 cloves of garlic
8 teaspoons of freshly ground
black pepper
2 cups red wine
water, salt as necessary

This is a very old pepper dish, as it used to be prepared in the ancient kilns at the time of Brunelleschi. The recipe was found in the house of an old Impruneta family. Originally, there were no tomatoes in Italy, so that these are a later addition.

Take a deep pan (earthenware if possible), and into this put the meat, cut into large cubes, the garlic, trimmed at top and bottom and then cut into little pieces, the tomatoes, salt and pepper. Barely cover with cold water and let it all cook slowly over a moderate heat. (If the water is all used up, add boiling water, a little at a time). After two hours, add the wine and continue cooking. (Put a lid on but leave a wooden spoon in at the edge of the pan so that it is not completely covered). After a further two hours, all the liquid should be absorbed. Do not add any fat.

Stracotto alla fiorentina / Florentine style braised beef

1 kg (2 pounds) beef
2 kg (4 pounds) onions
500 g (1 pound) tomatoes
3 carrots
2 cloves of garlic
1 stick of celery
8 leaves basil
1 glassful (1 cup) red wine
4 tablespoons (1/4 cup) extra
virgin olive oil
salt and pepper to taste

Pound together the garlic, salt and pepper. Make small incisions in the meat and insert the pounded garlic. Tie up the meat so that it stays in shape, then put it into a casserole with a little oil and let it brown for about 20 minutes. Finely chop the scraped and washed carrots, the celery, the onions, and a handful of basil leaves.
Put the vegetables and basil in an earthenware casserole with four tablespoonfuls of oil, add salt, and cook for half an hour on a moderate heat, then add the wine and tomatoes. Cook for a further 15 minutes, pass it all through a sieve and add this pureed sauce to the meat. Continue cooking for about four hours, adding boiling stock if the cooking liquid starts to dry out. When the meat is ready, remove the string used to tie it up, and slice it fairly thickly. Serve, with some of the sauce poured over it.
Cook some penne pasta "al dente" (i.e. still fairly firm). Strain the pasta, put it into a frying pan and toss it in the remaining sauce over a high heat.

Cristoforo Munari, Still life with ham, bread and cardoon, Florence, Pitti Palace (in storage)

Risotto con cardi e pancetta / Cardoon and bacon risotto

700 g (1 ½ pounds) cardoons,
previously boiled
500 g (1 pound) rice
150 g (5 oz) bacon
4 tablespoons (2 oz) grated grana-
padano cheese
½ litre (2 cups) veal stock
½ cup extra virgin olive oil
parsley
salt and pepper to taste

Slice the cardoons diagonally about 2 cm thick. Finely chop a handful of parsley, and put half of this in a saucepan together with two tablespoonfuls of oil and the bacon, previously cut into little cubes.
Fry lightly for a few minutes, and then add the sliced cardoons. Stir, and cook over a gentle heat, adding a ladleful of stock. When the liquid is absorbed and the cardoons start to soften, add the rice and fry lightly, stirring continually. Start cooking the risotto, stirring and adding boiling stock. Season with salt and pepper.
Take the risotto off the heat and then mix in the cheese and the remaining parsley. Let it stand a few minutes and then serve very hot.

Pane al formaggio / Cheese bread

350 g (3 cups) flour
150 g (5 oz) parmesan
150 g (5 oz) groviera cheese
3 eggs
150 g (5 oz) butter
yeast
½ glassful (1/3 cup) milk

Dissolve the yeast in the lukewarm milk and then pour this into the flour made into a well on the pastry board. Mix the two together and add the melted butter, three whole eggs and the finely grated cheeses. Knead well and then put it into a cake tin lined with oven-proof paper.
Let it rise for two hours before baking it in the oven for 35 minutes at 160° C. (320 F.). It is also possible to add crumbled sausages, or else nuts, or olives.

Cardi all'uovo / Cardoons with eggs

1 cardoon
2 lemons
1 tablespoon flour
2 eggs
100 g (4 oz) single cream
1 tablespoon grated parmesan
nut-sized piece of butter
a pinch of nutmeg
salt and pepper to taste

Clean the cardoon discarding the outside part, the leaves and the root. Cut the stalks into pieces removing the stringy bits, the hard fibres and the inside skin. After this, plunge the cardoon pieces in water acidulated with lemon juice to stop them turning black.

Mix the flour with a little cold water, beating it with a fork to smooth out any lumps, and add the juice of a lemon. Put about two litres of water into a saucepan, add the diluted flour, season with salt, and bring to the boil. Add the rinsed cardoon and when it all starts to boil again, turn down the heat as low as possible, cover, and cook for about an hour and a half until the cardoon is tender (15 minutes in a pressure cooker).

Pre-heat the oven to 200 C.(390 F.). Put the drained cardoon into a buttered ovenproof dish. Break the eggs into a bowl, add the cream and the parmesan and season with salt, pepper and a grating of nutmeg. Blend well, and pour over the warm cardoon.

Put the dish into the pre-heated oven for five or six minutes until the eggs have thickened to a creamy consistency.

Cristoforo Munari, Still life with pheasant, flask and eggs, Florence, Pitti Palace (in storage)

Crostini di fegatini di fagiano / Pheasant liver crostini

300 g (10 oz) pheasant liver
1 tablespoon (1/2 oz) butter
1 medium onion
1 teaspoon anchovy paste
1 tablespoon of capers
2 dl (1 cups) stock
2 tablespoons extra virgin olive oil
wine (Vin santo)
a pinch of salt

Fry the finely chopped onion very gently in a little oil and a tablespoonful of water until soft.

Add the cleaned and minced liver, season with salt and let the flavours mingle for two or three minutes. Before taking the sauce off the heat, add a little wine, let it evaporate, and then add a nut-sized piece of butter.

Put the prepared liver in the blender, together with the capers and the anchovy paste, and process it quickly.

Lightly toast some thin slices of Tuscan bread, dip them quickly in the stock, spread them with the sauce, and serve as an appetizer.

Fagiano alla panna / Pheasant with cream

1 pheasant
250 g (½ pound) chicken liver
dried mushrooms(1 oz)
½ glass (1/3 cup) cognac
½ litre (2 cups) single cream
50 g (2 oz) butter
salt and pepper to taste
rice pilaf as accompaniment

Clean the pheasant very well (and reserve the liver).

Cut the pheasant into pieces, and brown it in the butter together with its own liver and the chicken liver. Put the mushrooms in lukewarm water to soften them. When the pheasant starts to turn brown, pour the cognac over it, and let this evaporate. Take everything out of the pan, and mince the livers.

Mince the well-drained mushrooms, and add these to the liver and the cooking juices in the pan. Add the pheasant pieces and the cream, and cook thoroughly.

Prepare the rice pilaf (400 g - 1 pound), and serve the pheasant on top of the rice with the cooking-juice sauce poured over it.

Some of the sauce should be served separately at the table in a sauce boat.

*M*armellata di arance e limoni / *O*range and lemon marmalade

1 kg (2 pounds) oranges
2 lemons
800 g (3 ½ cups) sugar
vanilla

Use oranges and lemons which have not been chemically treated (i.e. unsprayed). Immerse the fruit in water and then wash carefully. Quarter each fruit, get rid of the seeds, and cut the peel and pulp into very tiny pieces.

Put the tiny bits of fruit into a pan together with two glasses of water. (First weigh the empty pan so as to be able to calculate the exact weight of the fruit mixture after the first cooking phase).

Cook the fruit over a very low heat for 40 minutes, counting from the time it starts to boil. The liquid should evaporate almost completely. At the end of this first phase, weigh the contents of the pan and add 800 grams (3 _ cups) of sugar for every kilogram (2 pounds) of the mixture (and decimal weight in this proportion).

Cook it again for 20 minutes (always counting from the moment it starts to boil). Be careful that the marmalade does not stick to the bottom of the pan.

To make sure that it is the right consistency, spread a small spoonful of the marmalade on to a plate, and put this in the freezer for a few minutes. If it forms a thin skin, this means the marmalade is ready.

When it has finished cooking, add a little vanilla flavouring. Let it cool a few moments. Fill the previously warmed jars very nearly to the brim. Close them hermetically and turn them upside down until they are cold. In this way they are automatically sterilized.

Camillo Berti, *Poulterer,* Florence Uffizi Gallery, Vasari's passage

Pollo con i funghi / Chicken with mushrooms

1 free-range chicken, weighing
about 1 kg (2 pounds)
500 g (1 pound) small firm
porcini mushrooms
1 small glassful (½ cup) dry white
wine
2 tablespoons extra virgin olive
oil
a little flour
1 small onion
1 glassful (1 cup) stock
calamint
salt and pepper to taste

Singe the chicken and divide it into eight pieces. Wash and dry them, and flour lightly, shaking each piece to get rid of any excess flour. Peel and finely chop the onion. Heat up the oil in a large non-stick frying pan, and brown the chicken pieces. Lower the heat and keep turning the chicken so that each piece browns evenly. Season with salt and pepper, and when the chicken is brown, add the onion. Continue stirring, being careful not to burn the onion, and when this starts to turn colour, pour on the wine. Let it evaporate and then add the stock. Cover, and let it all cook for about three quarters of an hour. Look at it every now and then, and if necessary add a few spoonfuls of stock.

Clean the mushrooms, cutting off the ends of the stalks and scraping with a knife to get rid of any dirt.

Slice thinly, and add to the pan ten minutes before taking the chicken off the heat. Season with salt and pepper to taste, and add a few leaves of calamint.

Cover, let it cook well, and serve very hot.

Pollo nel pangrattato / Bread-crumbed chicken

1 chicken, cut into pieces
100 g (4 oz) breadcrumbs
1 lemon
salt and pepper to taste

Mix the breadcrumbs with the grated lemon rind, salt and pepper, and put it all into a plastic bag.

Wash and dry the chicken pieces, and put them into the bag, a few at a time, shaking so that the chicken is well coated with breadcrumbs.

Put the chicken pieces into a baking dish, without seasoning, and cook them in the oven for about 40 minutes until they have a golden crust.

Nicola van Houbraken, *Vegetables, oysters and wine,* Florence, Pitti Palace (in storage)

*R*ibollita / *F*lorentine vegetable soup

½ savoy cabbage
1 red cabbage
1 small bundle of chard
450 g (1 pound) of dried white
beans (cannellini)
2 onions
1 clove of garlic
2 potatoes
2 carrots
2 sticks of celery
2 tablespoons of tomato puree
300 g (10 oz) stale home-made
bread
8 tablespoons extra virgin olive
oil
salt and pepper to taste

Because this soup involves a lot of work, it came to be prepared in large amounts, so that it was re-heated the following day, or for days after that - hence the name "ribollita", i.e. "reboiled".

Soften the beans by soaking in two litres of cold water, boil them and salt lightly when cooked. Drain, and pass three quarters of the cooked beans through a sieve, afterwards putting them back into the water in which they were cooked. Put aside the remaining whole beans.

Brown one very finely chopped onion and the garlic in 8 tablespoonfuls of oil, and as soon as the onion has turned colour, add two tablespoonfuls of tomato puree, diluted in a glassful of cold water. Add the carrots and celery, cut into very tiny pieces, then the cabbages and chard, cut into strips, and the thinly sliced peeled potatoes. Add salt and pepper to taste, cook for ten minutes, and then add the pureed beans with their cooking water. Continue cooking everything for about an hour.

When the vegetables are well done, add the sliced bread, the whole beans which were put aside, and mix it all together. Pour the soup into a soup tureen and serve with a drizzle of extra virgin olive oil.

Slice the other onion into very thin rounds and soak these in a little bowl of cold water for an hour, ready to serve separately with the soup.

Riso con il cavolfiore / Rice with cauliflower

1 small cauliflower
100 g (4 oz) grated parmesan
350 g (12 oz) rice
3 tablespoons (2 oz) butter
salt to taste
500 g (1 pound) white sauce
(made with 3 tablespoons butter,
3 tablespoons flour, 2 cups milk,
salt, nutmeg)

Prepare the white sauce: dissolve the flour in the butter in a saucepan, and add the milk, a little at a time, stirring to prevent any lumps. Season with salt, and when the sauce is ready, add a pinch of nutmeg as flavouring.

Wash and boil the cauliflower.

Prepare the rice pilaf: lightly fry a chopped onion in 50 g of butter (2 oz). When the onion has softened add the rice, let it brown for a minute, then add half a litre (2 cups) of stock and cook it in a covered dish in the oven for 20 minutes at 200 C..(390 F.). When all the above ingredients are ready, i.e. rice, white sauce and cauliflower, carefully butter a heat-resistant dish and put in a layer of cauliflower tips, and a second layer of rice pilaf, seasoned with the grated parmesan. Cover with a layer of white sauce, dot with butter and put the dish in the oven.

Cook at 180 C. (350 F.) until there is a thin light brown skin on top.

Cavolfiore aromatico / Aromatic cauliflower

1 cauliflower
2 tablespoons finely chopped
rosemary
2 cloves of garlic
1 small red chilli
3 tablespoons extra virgin olive
oil
3 tablespoons tomato puree
water as necessary (1/4 cup)

Divide up all the cauliflower tips, wash and rinse well but do not dry them. Put the cauliflower tips into a saucepan with a little oil and add the peeled garlic clove, the chopped rosemary and the chilli, cut into very tiny pieces. Brown for 10 minutes, and add the tomato puree diluted with two tablespoonfuls of water. Continue cooking for another 20 minutes, adding a little water if necessary.

Serve as an accompaniment around roast or boiled meat.

Cardi gratinati al forno / Cardoon browned in the oven

*1 cardoon weighing about 2 kg
(4 pounds)
2 lemons
2 tablespoons flour
3 tablespoons butter
2 cups of meat stock
2 tablespoons fresh breadcrumbs*

Clean the cardoon, and cut the stalks into pieces about 10 cm long, discarding filaments and skin. Put the pieces into water acidulated with lemon juice to prevent them turning black.

Fill a large pan with water, and put it on to boil. Dissolve two tablespoonfuls of flour in a cup of cold water containing the juice of a lemon, and add this to the boiling water. Put in the prepared cardoon and cook over a moderate heat until tender (one and a half to two hours). Drain the cardoon when cooked, and keep it covered.

Melt 50 g (2 oz) of butter in a small pan, add a tablespoonful of sieved flour, and continue stirring over a moderate heat until it starts to turn a light colour. Add the stock, bring to the boil and continue cooking over a very low heat, stirring all the time.

Butter a large ovenproof dish, put in the cooked cardoon, pour the sauce over it, sprinkle with breadcrumbs and dot with butter.

Put the dish in the pre-heated oven and bake for about 20 minutes at 200° C. (390 F.) until a golden crust has formed.

Willem van Aelst, *Still life of vegetables and sheep's head*, Florence, Pitti Palace, Palatine Gallery

Trippa alla fiorentina / Tripe, Florentine style

1 kg (2 pounds) veal tripe
300 g (10 oz) tomato puree
3 tablespoons extra virgin olive oil
2 onions, 2 carrots
2 sticks of celery, 1 clove of garlic
rosemary, parsley
6 tablespoons grated parmesan
a few tablespoons of stock
salt and pepper to taste

Rinse the tripe and then put it in salted boiling water together with one carrot, one celery stick, one chopped onion and a handful of parsley. When the water comes back to the boil, adjust the heat to its lowest setting, and continue cooking for about an hour and a half.

When the tripe is done, let it cool until tepid, and in the meantime pound together one onion, one carrot, a celery stick, a clove of garlic and some rosemary. Heat up the oil in a deep heavy pan over a moderate heat and soften the pounded herbs and vegetables, stirring with a wooden spoon.

Cut the tripe into strips and add it to the pan, turn up the heat and let all the flavours mingle, stirring often. After about half an hour, when the tripe starts to stick to the bottom of the pan, add salt, pepper and the tomato puree. Cover and continue cooking for at least an hour, stirring every now and then, and adding a spoonful of stock if necessary. Take the lid off the pan for the last few minutes of cooking if the sauce is not sufficiently reduced.

Tip the tripe on to a dish, and serve it very hot, sprinkled with the grated parmesan.

Coratella con i carciofi / Coratella with artichokes

1 "coratella" of lamb (see under)
1 sprig of sage
2 cloves of garlic
2 tablespoons of tomato sauce
4 artichokes
3 tablespoons oil
salt and pepper to taste

"Coratella" usually means the offal of the lamb, i.e. the liver, heart, spleen, lungs and kidneys. Clean all these carefully and cut into little pieces. Put them into a frying pan with the oil, the whole garlic cloves and the sage, and brown gently. Add the tomato sauce and a few spoonfuls of water if it is too dry.

Cook for about 20 minutes, and then take the pieces of meat out of the pan, and put in the prepared and cleaned artichokes, cut into quarters. If necessary, add a little more water. Cover, and cook for about a quarter of an hour. Put the meat pieces back into the pan, and serve.

Visciolato / Morello liqueur

500 g (1 pound) (morello)
cherries
1 teaspoon cinnamon
nutmeg
grated rind of one lemon
250 g (1 cup) sugar
1 cup white wine
1/3 cup alcohol for liqueur

Dry the cherries in the sun, and when they are ready, grind them, including their stones. Add cinnamon, nutmeg, grated lemon rind, sugar and white wine, and let it all ferment

for 40 days. At the end of this time, filter the liquid and let it stand. If it is less then 14° - 15°, add a little liqueur alcohol.

Nicaise Bernaerts, *Fowl and mushrooms,* Florence, Pitti Palace (in storage)

Zuppa di funghi / Mushroom soup

800 g (2 pounds) wild mushrooms (ceps)
2 cloves of garlic
4 ripe "San Marzano" tomatoes
4 slices of Tuscan bread
2 tablespoons of extra virgin olive oil
1 tablespoon of calamint
1 teaspoon salt
½ teaspoon pepper

Prepare the mushrooms (ceps) by scraping them with a knife and wiping them with a damp cloth (but do not wash them). Cut off the ends of the stalks. Thinly slice the mushrooms, and peel and finely chop the tomatoes, removing the seeds.

Heat up the oil in a casserole and brown the peeled garlic cloves, then add the mushrooms and the calamint and season with salt and pepper. Let the flavours mingle for a few minutes in the oil, on a high heat. Add the chopped tomatoes and a litre (4 cups) of hot water, and when the soup starts to boil, turn down the heat, cover, and continue cooking for about a quarter of an hour. Toast the bread slices, arrange them in a soup tureen, pour on the boiling hot soup and let it stand for a few minutes before serving.

Patè di fagiano di Annamaria / Annamaria's pheasant paté

1 pheasant, quartered, without its liver
1 medium-sized onion, 1 carrot, celery, parsley
sage, garlic, rosemary
extra virgin olive oil
250 g (1 cup) fresh cream
3 or 4 sheets of gelatine
Marsala (wine), salt and pepper

Brown the pheasant quarters in oil, season with salt and pepper. Separately, chop the onion, carrot, celery, parsley and two ripe tomatoes, and boil all these in a little water for 40 minutes.

Take the pheasant out of the pan and carefully remove all bones. Pound together the garlic, rosemary and sage, and fry lightly. Put the pheasant back in the same pan, let the flavours mingle, pour on the Marsala and blend the pheasant and herbs, whisking them together.

Strain off a little of the vegetable stock, and dissolve in it three or four sheets of gelatine (depending on the weight of the pheasant). Combine all the ingredients, and when they are completely cold, add 250 g (1 cup) of whipped cream.

Serve with little squares of toasted garlic bread.

Pietro Navarra, *Game, mushrooms and pomegranates,* Florence, Poggio Imperiale, Villa Medicea

Zuppa d'orzo con i funghi / Barley soup with wild mushrooms (ceps)

250 g (½ pound) pearl barley
400 g (1 pound) small firm wild
mushrooms (ceps)
1 litre (4 cups) stock
2 tablespoons of extra virgin olive oil
1 medium onion
2 cloves of garlic
calamint
salt and pepper

Lightly scrape the mushrooms with a small knife, and wipe off any earth with a damp cloth, having first removed the earthy ends of the stalks. Thinly slice the mushroom caps and put them aside. Mince the onion and one garlic clove.

Heat up a tablespoonful of oil in a casserole and soften the minced onion and garlic over a moderate heat. When they start to turn colour, add the minced mushroom stalks, stir, and fry lightly for a few minutes. Add the barley, mix, and let the flavours mingle for two minutes before adding the boiling stock. Cover, and cook for an hour.

Separately, heat up the other tablespoonful of oil in a frying pan, and brown a peeled and crushed clove of garlic. When the garlic starts to turn colour, take it out of the pan and tip in the sliced mushroom caps. Season with salt and pepper, and cook for about ten minutes on a gentle heat, stirring lightly and carefully. When the barley has finished cooking, add the contents of the frying pan containing the sliced mushrooms. Season again with salt to taste, and continue cooking for a few minutes, adding more stock if necessary.

Flavour with a few leaves of calamint, and serve very hot.

Fagiano o faraona con i funghi / *Pheasant or guinea fowl with wild mushrooms*

1 bird, weighing approx. 1 kg (2 pounds)
500 g (1 pound) small firm mushrooms
1 scant glass of dry white wine
2 tablespoons extra virgin olive oil
a little (2 tablespoons) flour
1 small onion
1 glass (½ cup) stock
calamint
salt and pepper

Singe the bird and cut it up into 8 pieces. Wash under running water, dry and flour lightly, shaking each piece to get rid of any excess flour.

Chop the onion very finely.

Heat the oil in a large, non-stick frying pan, and brown the pheasant pieces over a moderate heat. Turn frequently so that they brown evenly.

Season with salt and pepper, and when the pheasant pieces are well browned, add the chopped onion. Continue stirring, being careful not to burn the onion, and as soon as the latter starts to turn colour, pour on the wine. When this has evaporated, add the stock, cover, and continue cooking for about three quarters of an hour, adding a few spoonfuls of stock, if necessary. Scrape the mushrooms with a small knife and cut off the ends of the stalks. Remove any dirt by wiping the mushrooms with a damp cloth, then slice them thinly. Ten minutes before taking the pheasant off the heat, add the sliced mushrooms to the pan, season with salt and pepper to taste, add a few calamint leaves, cover, and heat through to continue cooking.

Anonymous Roman Artist, *Fruit and vegetables,* Florence, Pitti Palace (in storage)

Zuppa di zucca con i funghi / Pumpkin soup with mixed wild mushrooms

750 g (1 ½ pound) peeled
pumpkin
100 g (4 oz) Emmental cheese
3 shallots
500 g (1 pound) mixed wild
mushrooms
500 g (2 cups) milk
2 cups vegetable stock
4 small slices of Tuscan bread
2 bay leaves
3 juniper berries
extra virgin olive oil (3
tablespoons)
salt
grated parmesan

Cut the pumpkin into little pieces, and cook for 20 minutes in a saucepan containing the milk, vegetable stock, bay leaves and the peeled and halved shallots.

Salt lightly. Take out the bay leaves and some of the shallot halves (putting aside one or two for decoration).

Liquidise the remaining contents of the pan. Put the cleaned and sliced wild mushrooms into a frying pan together with two or three tablespoonfuls of oil, the crushed juniper berries and a little salt. Cook for 15 minutes over a moderate heat.

Pour the pumpkin puree into little individual bowls, alternately with the mushrooms, small cubes of toasted bread and the grated cheese. Slice the shallots which were put aside, and sprinkle them on top. Put the soup under the grill for a few seconds, and drizzle with a little olive oil before serving.

Asparagi al gorgonzola / Asparagus with gorgonzola

A bundle of asparagus
200 g (7 oz) gorgonzola cheese
200 g (1 cup) cream
nut-sized piece of butter
salt

Clean the asparagus and then either boil or steam it, previously discarding the woody part of the stalks. Place the asparagus carefully in a buttered heat-resistant dish. Quickly process together the gorgonzola with the cream to make a fairly thin sauce. Season with salt. Pour the sauce over the asparagus, and brown it in the oven for a few minutes. The sauce should only just turn a light gold and still have a creamy texture.

Insalata di ovoli / Mushroom salad

250 g (½ pound) small, fresh and
firm mushrooms (ovoli)
100 g (4 tabelspoons) parmesan
1 small white truffle
salt
extra virgin olive oil
lemons
nepitella leaves (calamint)

To clean the mushrooms, remove the earth round the stalks with a small sharp knife, and wipe the mushrooms with a damp cloth, but do not wash them. Slice thinly letting the slices fall into a large shallow dish. Use a truffle slicer to scatter plenty of parmesan flakes over the mushrooms. Season with oil, a little lemon juice and salt. Mix it all together very carefully. Scatter generously with flakes of white truffle, and garnish with a few leaves of calamint.

Aspic di frutti rossi alla melagrana / Red fruit jelly with pomegranate

2 pomegranates
500 g (1 pound) of mixed red
fruit (raspberries, strawberries
and redcurrants)
200 g (1 cup) sugar
2 dl (1 cup)prosecco wine
3 dl (1 cup) water
25 g (1 oz) sheet gelatine
juice and peel of 1 lemon
peel of 1 orange
3 cloves
a few leaves of fresh mint

Bring to the boil the water containing the sugar, lemon juice and peel, orange peel and cloves.
Meanwhile, soak the gelatine in cold water. Take the spicy flavoured water off the heat and then add the drained and squeezed gelatine. Strain in all through a sieve, add the prosecco, mix well and let it cool a little. Peel the pomegranates and mix the seeds with the other fruit, also adding the mint leaves. Now take a cake mould and pour in a thin layer of the liquid, prepared as above, and put it in the fridge to cool completely. When it has set, arrange all the fruit on top and carefully pour on the rest of the liquid. Put it in the fridge for at least three hours. Very quickly dip the mould into hot water and then turn the jelly out on to a rectangular plate. Serve it garnished with mint leaves and pomegranate seeds.

Pannacotta con salsa di fragole / "Cooked cream" dessert with strawberry sauce

250 g (1 cup) fresh cream
250 g (1 cup) fresh whole milk
80 g (3 oz) vanilla-flavoured
icing sugar
10 g (½ oz) gelatine

For the sauce:
200 g (8 oz) ripe strawberries
40 g (4 tablespoons) sugar
a few small green candied
cherries or a few small mint
leaves to garnish

Soften the gelatine in a small bowl of cold water.
Put the cream and icing sugar into a saucepan on the hotplate and mix well to dissolve the sugar without letting it all come to the boil. At the same time, in another pan, dissolve the drained and squeezed sheets of gelatine in the hot milk. Carefully mix together the contents of both pans and then distribute into four small moulds. Put these moulds into the fridge for three or four hours, or even overnight. Just before serving the dessert, wash the strawberries under running water and dry them on kitchen paper. Process them in the mixer to make a smooth runny sauce and divide this between four small dessert plates. Tip the cooked cream out of the moulds on to the strawberry sauce on each plate, and decorate with a few small leaves of mint. The cooked cream comes out of the moulds easily if they are quickly dipped in boiling water, dried, and then turned upside down.

Nicola van Houbraken, *Vegetables,* Florence, Pitti Palace (in storage)

Acquacotta di primavera / Light spring soup

200 g (7 oz) shelled peas
150 g (5 oz) fresh shelled broad beans
4 small artichokes
200 g (7 oz) wild asparagus
300 g (10 oz) beetroot
1 carrot
1 stick of celery
2 cloves of garlic
4 sage leaves
2 tablespoons extra virgin olive oil
1 lemon
4 eggs
4 slices of homemade Tuscan bread
4 tablespoons of grated sheep's cheese, or parmesan

Wash and cut the asparagus into pieces, discarding the hard bits. Clean the artichokes, cut them into eight segments and put these into a tureen full of water acidulated with lemon juice. Clean, and roughly chop the beetroot. Clean the carrot and slice it thinly, also the celery. Peel and slice the garlic cloves, having first removed the little core at the bottom, and then put the garlic into a saucepan, together with the oil and sage leaves. When the garlic starts to turn colour, add all the vegetables and let them soften to bring out the flavour. Season with salt and pepper. Pour on one and a half litres of boiling water, cover, and cook over a moderate heat for 20 minutes. Toast the bread slices, flavour with garlic if liked, and put them in a soup tureen. When the vegetables are soft, turn down the heat to its lowest setting. Break the eggs one at a time on to a dish, and tip them into the saucepan as for poached eggs. Let the eggs cook for two or three minutes, and then take them out with a slotted spoon and place them on the slices of bread. Pour on the soup, and sprinkle it with grated parmesan (or sheep's cheese).

Let it rest for a few minutes before serving.

Intingolo di carciofi / Tasty artichoke dish

400 g (1 pound) artichokes
1 large shallot
oil, salt, white pepper
1 teacup of grated parmesan cheese
1 cup mayonnaise.

Roughly chop the artichokes, finely chop the shallot, season with salt and pepper, and cook them in a frying pan, with the oil. Add the parmesan and mayonnaise (plus a little milk if the pan contents are too dry). Place all the ingredients in a deep heat-resistant dish and put this in the oven for a few minutes.

Keep the dish on a plate warmer when serving, with "crostini" (small cubes of toast) as accompaniment.

Risotto agli asparagi / Asparagus risotto

300 g (12 oz) Arborio or Carnaroli rice
a bundle of asparagus
1 onion
80 g (3 ½ oz) butter
½ litre (2 cups) good quality stock
plenty of grated parmesan
breadcrumbs
salt and pepper

For the white sauce:
60 g (5 tablespoons) butter
60 g (5 tablespoons) flour
½ litre (3 cups) milk
nutmeg (½ teaspoon)
salt and pepper

Chop the onion very finely and soften by frying gently in 40 g of butter. When the onion is ready, add the rice, plus a little salt, and mix well so that the rice is well flavoured. Add the boiling stock, cover, and put it all in the oven to continue cooking at 250°C. (480 F.). Do not stir it any more. When the stock has been absorbed, the rice will be cooked exactly right. Take it out of the oven, add the rest of the butter, plus the grated cheese, and lift up the rice grains with a fork. Meanwhile, steam the asparagus and prepare the white sauce: cook together the sieved flour and melted butter over a moderate heat, mixing well to form a roux, then add the milk, a little at a time, and cook thoroughly. Season with salt and pepper, and add a pinch of nutmeg.

Butter a deep ovenproof dish, sprinkle it with breadcrumbs, and put in a compact, even layer of asparagus, cut into little segments (only use the tender bits). Cover the asparagus with the rice, spread in one layer, and pour the white sauce over the rice. Dot with butter, and put the dish into the oven for 15-20 minutes at 200° C.(390 F.) until well browned. Let it rest a few minutes before serving.

Anonymous artist of Lucca, *Two vases of flowers, fruit and artichoke,* Pisa, Scuola Normale Superiore, Florentine Galleries (in storage)

Fegatelli con il finocchietto selvatico / Liver of pork with wild fennel

400 g (14 oz) sliced pork liver
caul of pork
2 cloves of garlic
wild fennel
(½ cup)extra virgin olive oil
salt and pepper

Remove any excess fat from the liver slices, and turn them in a mixture of finely minced garlic, wild fennel crushed to a powder, salt and pepper.

Meanwhile, put the caul to soften for at least half an hour in a bowl of tepid water. Stretch it out carefully on a large flat surface, and cut it into squares large enough to contain a slice of liver. Wrap each slice up in one of these squares, and fasten with a stalk of wild fennel.

Cook the liver with the olive oil in a covered saucepan over a moderate heat. Add a few spoonfuls of stock if necessary.

Maialino al forno con finocchietto / Roast pork with fennel

1 very small joint of pork
generous amount of wild fennel
2 cloves of garlic
salt and pepper

Wash the meat and season it with the very finely chopped garlic, plenty of wild fennel, crushed to a powder, salt and pepper. Put it in a casserole with extra virgin olive oil, and cook it in a very slow oven.

Alternatively, sprinkle the joint generously with a mixture of finely chopped garlic, wild fennel, salt and pepper, and roast it in the oven on a turn spit.

Verdura al finocchietto / Vegetable dish with fennel

500 g (1 pound)small boiled
turnips
garlic
wild fennel
extra virgin olive oil
salt and pepper

Finely chop the boiled and well squeezed turnips, and gently fry them to soften in a frying pan containing a browned garlic clove. Together with the vegetable, put a generous amount of wild fennel in the pan, and season it all with salt and pepper.

Giovanna Garzoni, *Dish with beans,* Florence, Pitti Palace, Palatine Gallery

Insalata di fave / Broad bean salad

400 g (1 pound) broad beans
1 clove of garlic
2 sprigs of mint
extra virgin olive oil
salt and pepper

Cook the shelled beans "al dente", i.e. they must still be fairly firm (for about a quarter of an hour), and season them with the garlic, chopped fresh mint, salt, pepper, and plenty of olive oil.

Garmugia / Garmugia soup

500 g (1 pound) peas
1 kg (2 pounds) small tender broad beans
4 violet-coloured (globe) artichokes
500 g (1 pound) green asparagus
200 g (7 oz) minced veal
juice of half a lemon
5 or 6 spring onions
2 tablespoons extra virgin olive oil
1 slice of bacon
4 slices of home-made bread
2 tablespoons grated parmesan cheese
2 vegetable cubes
salt and pepper

Shell the peas and broad beans and put them to soak in cold water. Cut off the artichoke stalks, leaving just a small piece, discard the hard leaves, cut off the tips and get rid of the whiskery part which may possibly be found in the middle. Cut the artichokes into little segments, and put these into water acidulated with lemon juice. Wash the asparagus and finely chop the tender parts. Finely slice the white part of the spring onions and put them in a saucepan with the oil and the bacon, cut into tiny cubes. Soften over a moderate heat, stirring often. When the contents of the pan start to turn colour, turn up the heat and add the crumbled minced meat. Continue browning, stirring frequently. When the meat is dry, add the peas, artichokes, beans and asparagus. Season with salt and pepper, and let the flavours mingle for a few minutes. Finally, add the vegetable cubes and half a litre of water.

Continue cooking for about three quarters of an hour.

When the soup has finished cooking, toast the bread slices and place them in four deep bowls.

Pour on the soup, and serve very hot, sprinkled with grated parmesan.

Mario de' Fiori, *Vase with caper flowers,* Florence, Pitti Palace (in storage)

Salsa vinagrette / Vinaigrette sauce

1 tablespoon capers
1 tablespoon chilli powder
tarragon, parsley
onion, chervil
2 tablespoons vinegar
6 tablespoons extra virgin olive
oil
salt and pepper

Chop the tarragon, parsley, chilli, onion and chervil very finely indeed, and add a tablespoonful of each to the minced capers.

Add the vinegar, oil, salt and pepper, and blend well.

Spaghettini saporiti / Savoury spaghetti

500 g (1 pound) "spaghettini"
200 g (7 oz) tuna fish
2 tablespoons capers
2 small fresh onions
a very small amount of chilli,
salt, oil

Mince the onions together with the chilli, and put them in a frying pan with a little oil. Fry lightly and then add the tuna fish and the capers. Cook for 10 minutes adding

two tablespoonfuls of the spaghetti cooking water. Cook the spaghetti until barely soft (al dente), and toss it in the pan together with the other ingredients.

Salsa di capperi / Caper sauce

2 tablespoons capers
1 lemon, parsley
extra virgin olive oil, salt

Mince the capers (possibly in the blender), add the lemon juice, a little finely chopped

parsley and enough oil to make a thick sauce. Season with salt to taste.

Anonymous artist, *Grapes and pumpkins,* Florence, Pitti Palace (in storage)

Gnocchi di zucca / Pumpkin tiny dumplings

1 kg (2 pounds) pumpkin
250 g (2 cups) flour
1 egg, nutmeg
50 g (2 oz) butter
2 tablespoons parmesan
sage, salt

Cut the pumpkin into segments, removing seeds and fibre, and then place the segments in a heat-proof dish, with the peel facing downwards. Put the dish into the pre-heated oven and cook the contents for about an hour at 180 C.(350 F.). After this, let the pumpkin cool a little, then remove the peel and pass the pulp through a finely-meshed vegetable sieve into a bowl. If the puree is too watery, put it on the stove to dry out a little, without adding any seasoning. Add the egg and nearly all the sieved flour, plus a grating of nutmeg and a pinch of salt. Put the mixture on to a pastry board and work it into a smooth dough with an even texture.

Cut off a third and form it into a little roll about 1 cm in diameter. Cut off little pieces of about 2 cm and roll them round on the board. Make little ridges on each tiny dumpling using the prongs of a fork or the back of the grater, as for potato "gnocchi". Boil some water in a large saucepan and prepare the flavoured butter by frying it gently on a very low heat, together with the sage leaves. When the water boils, add salt and put in the "gnocchi". Let them boil for a few minutes, and when they rise to the surface of the water, take them out with a slotted spoon and season them with the sage-flavoured butter and the parmesan.

Tordi all'uva / Thrushes with grapes

10 thrushes
½ glass of extra virgin olive oil
10 black olives
4 cloves of garlic
1 sprig of sage
1 cup of white grapes, not too ripe
1 ripe tomato
a little stock
salt

Put the oil, olives, garlic cloves and sage into a casserole and brown lightly. When the garlic has just turned brown, immediately add the peeled and chopped tomato, the prepared and cleaned thrushes and the grapes.

Cook slowly, stirring often, and if necessary add a few tablespoonfuls of stock. Serve on slices of polenta.

Crostata di zucca / Pumpkin tart

For the short crust pastry:
200 g (7 oz) flour
1 egg yolk
70 g (2 ½ oz) sugar
150 g (5 oz) softened butter

For the filling:
500 g (1 pound) cooked yellow pumpkin
1 cup of cane sugar
2 eggs
1 cup of cream
1 cup of milk
a few drops of vanilla essence
1 teaspoon cinnamon
nutmeg
powdered ginger
1 tablespoon cognac
whipped cream to garnish

To prepare the short crust pastry, mix together the butter and sugar, add the egg yolk and finally the flour. Quickly work it all together, form it into a ball of dough and let it rest in the fridge, preferably overnight. To prepare the filling, pass the pumpkin through a sieve and carefully mix it with all the other ingredients. Line a hinged tart dish, 24 cm in diameter, with the short crust pastry and put in the prepared pumpkin mixture. Bake in the oven at 180° C. (350 F.) for 15 minutes, and then lower the temperature to 160°C. (320 F.) for a further 25 minutes. Let it cool and serve cold, decorated with whipped cream.

Gelo di mosto e mostarda (mostata) / Must jelly and "mostarda" preserve

½ litre must
50 g (2 oz) sugar
50 g (2 oz) corn flour (American cornstarch)
grape leaves

For the "mostarda" preserve:
whole almonds
sun-dried orange peel

Blend the corn flour with the sweetened and decanted new wine, cook it over a low heat, stirring constantly, with a wooden spoon, and then pour the mixture into terracotta moulds. When the jelly is well set, turn it out of the moulds on to some grape leaves.

The "mostarda" preserve is made by flavouring the must mixture as above with a pinch of sun-dried orange peel which has been crushed to a powder in a mortar. Add some whole almonds and then pour the "mostarda" into the moulds. Let it cool completely and then turn it out of the moulds on to a board covered with a clean table napkin and put the jelly preserve shapes out to dry in the sun.

Bartolomeo Bimbi, *Fruit and mushrooms,* Florence, Pitti Palace (in storage)

*S*ouflé di funghi e prosciutto / *H*am and mushroom soufflé

200 g (7 oz) mushrooms
50 g (2 oz) uncooked ham in one
slice
80 g (2 oz) butter
4 eggs
80 g (2 ½ oz) flour
250 g (1 cup) milk
nutmeg
salt and pepper

Discard the earthy part of the stems, wipe the mushrooms with a damp cloth and chop them very finely. Mince the ham having first removed the fat. Put the mushrooms in a frying pan with 20 g butter (2 tablespoons), season with salt and pepper, and cook gently until they have dried out. Heat the milk thoroughly, seasoning it with salt, pepper and a pinch of nutmeg.

Separately, melt 50 g (2 oz)of butter in a small heavy-based saucepan, add the sieved flour and cook for a minute, stirring at the same time. Add the milk and continue stirring until it comes to the boil. Take it off the heat, let it cool, and add the egg yolks, one at a time (keep the whites separately in a bowl).

Mix the mushrooms and the ham into the white sauce.

Use an electric beater to whip the egg whites, with a pinch of salt, until they are stiff, then using a rubber spatula, carefully add the whipped egg whites to the sauce mixture, folding them in from top to bottom. Butter a round ovenproof dish, 16 cm in diameter, and pour in the contents of the saucepan. Cook at 200° C. (390 F.) in a pre-heated oven for 3/4 of an hour, without opening the oven door during this time. Serve the soufflé the minute it is ready so that it does not sink down.

Porcini in teglia / Pan-cooked wild mushrooms

*8 medium-sized wild mushrooms
(ceps)
100 g (4 oz) raw ham, in one
slice
50 g (2 oz) butter
1 shallot
extra virgin olive oil
8 quails' eggs
finely chopped chervil*

Clean the mushrooms carefully, cut off the stalks and wipe the caps with a damp cloth. Cut the ham into cubes and put it in a frying pan with 20 g (1 oz) of butter, the thinly sliced mushroom stalks and a finely chopped shallot. Cook for 5-6 minutes.

Separately, cook the mushroom caps in a non-stick pan, adding two tablespoonfuls of oil. When they are soft, season with salt and keep them warm. Melt the rest of the butter in a large frying pan. Break the quails' eggs into the pan and cook them for two minutes.

Arrange the mushroom caps in a dish, put the eggs on top and also the mixture of chopped ham, shallots and mushroom stalks. Add a tablespoonful of very finely chopped chervil to flavour, and serve immediately.

Gelatina di melagrana / Pomegranate jelly

*2 kg (4 pounds) ripe
pomegranates
sugar
1 orange*

Peel the pomegranates, and remove the skins which separate the grains. Spin the grains in a centrifuge and collect the juice in a bowl. Weigh it and then pour it into a heavy-based pan. Add an equal weight of sugar to the pomegranate juice, plus the grated zest of an orange, and bring it to the boil. Continue cooking it, stirring often, until a few drops on a cold plate start to congeal very quickly. Pour the jelly into sterilised jars, closing them immediately.

Giacomo Fardella, *Fruit and flowers with figures,* Florence, Pitti Palace (in storage)

Coniglio alla chiantigiana / Rabbit, Chianti style

1 de-boned rabbit
150 g (6 oz) sliced bacon
400 g (1 pound) minced pork
and veal
100 g (3 ½ oz) cream
the soft part of a bread roll
1 tablespoon of pounded
rosemary and garlic
white wine
300 g (10 oz) of black and white
grapes
2 sage leaves
1 bay leaf
extra virgin olive oil
salt and pepper

Mix together in a bowl the minced meat, the inside of a bread roll, softened in milk and then well squeezed, the cream, salt and pepper. Open out the rabbit and hold it open on a table. Spread it with the pounded paste of rosemary and garlic, the bacon slices and the meat mixture, prepared as above. Roll up the rabbit and tie it shut. Cook it in the oven for about an hour, with a little oil, moistening it occasionally with white wine. When it has finished cooking, take the stuffed rabbit out of the dish, pour off nearly all the cooking juices, and to the remaining juicy sediment add the black and white grapes, plus the sage and bay leaves. Put the dish back into the oven until the grapes have split open. Pour this sauce over the rabbit, which has been carved into slices.

Frutta giulebbata / Caramelised fruit

3 apples, 3 pears, 3 oranges, 1
lemon
a few nut kernels
a few stoned plums
grapes if liked
pine nuts
peaches in season
sugar

Mix together the fruit, chopped into large pieces, including one orange with finely cut-up peel and the juice of two oranges. Add a tablespoonful of sugar for each fruit, and put it all in the oven to caramelise, in a heat-resistant dish. Serve with custard cream, made with the addition of lemon peel or mint.

Giovanni Pini, *Young man outside with food basket,* Florence, Pitti Palace (in storage)

Cialdoni / Cornets

80 g (3 oz) flour
30 g (3 tablespoons) sugar
20 g (2 tablespoons) butter
7 tablespoons chilled water

Mix together the sugar, the flour and the water. Add the butter and blend it all together to make a dough. A special gadget is need to cook the cornets. It consists of two metal discs which open out like scissors. Lightly butter these discs, and put a spoonful of dough on one of them. Shut the gadget so that the second disc covers the first one.

Put it on the hotplate and cook quickly on both sides. As soon as the cornet is a light brown colour, turn it out and immediately roll it up on itself into a cone shape, which will harden as it cools. Continue in this way until all the dough has been used up. Serve with whipped cream.

Brigidini / Aniseed biscuits

100 g (3 ½ oz) flour
120 g (3 oz) sugar
2 eggs
10 g (1 tablespoon) aniseed
pinch of salt

These little biscuits need a special gadget consisting of two iron parts called "forms" which take a small amount of dough in the middle, pressing it flat as it cooks.
Mix together all the ingredients to make a fairly firm dough, and work it for a few

minutes. Heat the iron forms on the stove, put a nut sized piece of dough in the middle, squeeze it between the forms and cook it on both sides. Continue cooking the biscuits in this way, one at a time, between the forms.

Roschette

200 g (7 oz) flour
100 g (3 ½ oz) icing sugar
100 g (3 ½ oz) almonds
80 g (3 oz) butter
30 g (1 oz) lard
2 eggs

Shell and skin the almonds and roast them until they turn nut brown, and then grind them quite finely.

Mix together the ground almonds, sugar and flour, and put this mixture on the work surface. Make a well in the centre, add one whole egg, and an extra yolk, plus the butter and the lard. Mix and work it together quickly into a ball of dough. Let it rest for a few hours.

Flour the rolling pin and roll the dough out to a thickness of about 1 cm and then cut out little shapes.

Place them on a buttered baking sheet and cook them in the oven.

Panforte / Spicy fruit and nut bread

100 g (3 ½ oz) acacia honey
300 g (7 oz) shelled sweet almonds
200 g (7 oz) nut kernels
150 g (5 oz) dried figs
150 g (5 oz) candied cedar
150 g (5 oz) candied pumpkin
150 g (5 oz)candied orange
150 g (5 oz)shelled hazelnuts
200 g (7 oz)icing sugar
50 g (2 oz) sweetened cocoa
15 g (1 tablespoon) cinnamon powder
15 g (1 tablespoon) clove mixture
white pepper
powdered coriander and nutmeg
oven paper to line the mould

Scald the almonds and nut kernels in boiling water, then peel and grind them, and dry them in a slow oven. Roast the hazelnuts, remove their skin by rubbing them with a cloth, and then chop them roughly.

Cut up the candied and dried fruit very finely, and mix everything together in a bowl. Sprinkle in the cocoa, the spices, with only half of the cinnamon powder, and mix well.

Separately, put the honey and 175 g (5 oz) of the icing sugar into a small concave-based saucepan (preferably a copper one), and blend well, using a wooden spoon.

Keep the pan on a very low heat for 10 minutes, then take it off the hotplate and add the chopped fruit and nuts, stirring to mix them in well. Line the sides and the base of a hinged mould 24 cm in diameter, butter it lightly, fill in the mixture and level it off.

Bake in a moderate oven (160 C. - 320 F.) for 30 - 40 minutes.

When it is cooked, let it cool completely, and then remove it from the mould and sprinkle with the remaining icing sugar and powdered cinnamon. Keep the spicy bread in a dry place, possibly wrapped in aluminium foil.

Anonymous artist, *Summer allegory,* Florence, Pitti Palace (in storage)

Zuppa di farro / Spelt soup

200 g (7 oz) spelt
500 g (1 pound) fresh red beans
or 300 g (10 oz) dried red beans
half an onion
1 small stick of celery
1 carrot
four sage leaves
a handful of marjoram
a sprig of rosemary
a pinch of powdered nutmeg and
cinnamon
2 cloves
100 g (3 ½ oz) uncooked ham cut
into cubes
150 g (5 oz) tomatoes
extra virgin olive oil
salt and pepper

Quickly wash the spelt. Put it in cold water to get rid of the dirt which will rise to the surface, and after eight hours soaking, rinse it through twice. Boil the beans for about two hours. (If using dried beans, these must also be soaked for about eight hours before cooking). Drain the beans and sieve them. Put aside the cooking water. Pound together the garlic, onion, sage, rosemary, marjoram and carrot, and lightly fry the pounded mixture in the olive oil, together with the cubed ham. Add the tomatoes, plus a pinch of spice, season with salt and pepper, and cook for 15 minutes, then rub it all through a sieve. Add the spelt, the bean puree and a little of the water used for cooking the beans. Stir, and continue cooking for 35 - 40 minutes, adding enough of the beans' cooking water to make a soup of a good consistency.

Serve with a swirl of extra virgin olive oil and a grinding of fresh pepper.

Minestra di farro / Spelt soup 2

200 g (7 oz) dried borlotti beans
150 g (5 oz) whole spelt
4 peeled tomatoes
a piece of ham rind
2 tablespoons extra virgin olive oil
1 small onion
1 stick of celery
1 carrot
1 clove of garlic
4 sage leaves
salt and pepper

Rinse the beans and then put them in lukewarm water to soak for about 8 hours. Before cooking them, rinse again and put them in a saucepan, cover them with cold water and bring this to the boil. As soon as it boils, season with salt, turn the heat down to its lowest setting, cover, and simmer the beans for two and a half hours. (They must be tender). Remove excess fat from the inside of the ham rind, and lightly scrape the outside rind. Scald it for a few minutes, drain, and add it to the beans.

Pound together the garlic, celery, onion, carrot and sage, then brown it all in a saucepan with a little oil. When this mixture starts to turn brown, add the peeled and finely chopped tomatoes, the cooked ham rind, also finely chopped, and cook it all for about ten minutes. Add the strained beans and some of their cooking water. Bring to the boil, season with salt and pepper to taste, and add the rinsed spelt. Continue cooking on a moderate heat for about three quarters of an hour. If the soup seems to be too thick, add a little more of the beans' cooking water.

Sformato di grano saraceno / Buckwheat soufflé

200 g (7 oz) buckwheat
half a litre (2 cups) vegetable stock
1 onion, 1 pepper, 2 cloves of garlic
2 eggs
100 g (3 ½ oz) sheep's cheese
thyme
extra virgin olive oil
salt and pepper

After washing and draining the buckwheat, grind it coarsely and soak it in the stock, together with the thyme. Slice the onion thinly, cut the washed pepper into strips and brown lightly in two tablespoonfuls of olive oil. Add the buckwheat, together with the stock, and cook over a moderate heat for 20 minutes so that all the liquid is absorbed. Add the egg yolks, salt and pepper to taste, and flavour it with the thyme. Whip the egg whites with a pinch of salt until stiff, and add them to the mixture. Put it all into a buttered baking pan, 26 cm in diameter, sprinkle with sheep's cheese, and cook in a pre-heated oven at 180 C. (350 F.) for 30-40 minutes.

Antonio Tanari, *Fish,* Poggio a Caiano, Villa Medicea, Florentine galleries (in storage)

Zuppa di pesce / Fish soup

800 g (2 pounds) John Dory fish
800 g (2 pounds) angler (frog)
fish
4 slices of smooth dogfish
4 large Dublin Bay prawns
600 g (1 ½ pounds) red mullet
4 small slices of skate
800 g (2 pounds) fish heads (can
be from various kinds of fish)
400 g (1 pound) cuttlefish
8 clams
8 small crabs
1 scant glass of extra virgin olive
oil
1/4 green pepper
1 kg (2 pounds) tomatoes
2 cloves of garlic
chopped parsley,
chilli
salt

The above list only serves to indicate the quantity and type of fish for this recipe, but substitutions and additions can be used according to availability and personal taste. Wash and dry all the fish. Put the washed, peeled and finely chopped tomatoes into a large frying pan.

Add the finely chopped garlic cloves, the chopped pepper, strips of cuttlefish and a small piece of sharp chilli. Finally add the oil, season with salt, mix, and put the frying pan on the stove. Cook the contents for about a quarter of an hour. When the tomatoes have softened and shrunk somewhat, add the fish in cooking order: first of all, put in the prawns and the angler fish. After a few minutes, add all the fish, cut into slices, the clams and the small crabs. Finally, after another five minutes, add the red mullets. Season, and continue cooking for a further five or six minutes.

To keep shape and consistency, it is better not to stir the fish too much whilst cooking. Sprinkle with chopped parsley, and the soup is ready.

Serve it very hot with thin slices of toast.

Calamari ripieni / Small stuffed squids

800 g (2 pounds) of squids, all the same size if possible
1 tablespoon fresh breadcrumbs
2 tablespoons grated sheep's cheese
1 egg
2 tablespoons extra virgin olive oil
400 g (1 pound) tomato pulp
2 cloves of garlic
dry white wine
parsley, red chilli
salt and pepper

Detach the tentacles of the squids from the "bags" (i.e. the soft body part), carefully clean tentacles and the bags, both inside and out. Rinse well in plenty of water, mince the tentacles and put them in a bowl. Add the parsley, the finely chopped garlic clove, the breadcrumbs, sheep's cheese and the whole egg. Season with salt and plenty of pepper and mix well. Dry the bags with kitchen paper, also on the inside, and fill them two thirds full with the prepared mixture. Use a toothpick to fasten the opening.

Heat the oil in a pan, and brown the other peeled and crushed garlic clove, plus the chilli, over a moderate heat. Add the little stuffed "bags", and brown lightly. Pour on white wine to moisten, and when this has evaporated, add the tomato pulp. Season with salt, cover, and continue cooking for one hour, turning the squids round from time to time.
Serve hot.

Totani in zimino / Squid in vegetable sauce

1 kg (2 pounds) beetroots
500 g (1 pound) of squids
1 onion
1 stick of celery
tomato puree
2 cloves of garlic
a handful of parsley
red chilli
dry white wine
extra virgin olive oil
salt

Clean and wash the squids and cut them into strips.
Fry together the finely chopped onion and celery in olive oil, and when the onion has turned brown, add the sliced squids. Brown gently for a few minutes, then add the wine and let it evaporate. Add the tomato puree, and continue cooking over a moderate heat until the fish is tender. Peel and wash the beetroots and cook them in a very little water. When they are done, squeeze them, cut them up roughly, and brown them in oil with the garlic. When the beetroots are brown, remove the garlic and add them to the squids. Season with salt to taste, and add the whole chilli and the chopped parsley. Simmer slowly for 5-6 minutes, stirring often to prevent it all sticking to the bottom of the pan. At the end of this time, make sure that the squids are tender, and remove the chilli.

Bartolomeo Bimbi, *Shells,* Siena, Province Palace

Pasta e fagioli con le vongole / Pasta with beans and clams

200 g (7 oz) of a short type of
pasta
200 g (7 oz) dried beans
(cannellini)
1 kg (2 pounds) of ordinary
clams
3 cloves of garlic
1 bay leaf
extra virgin olive oil
salt and pepper

Put the beans into lukewarm water, and soak them for several hours. After this, drain and rinse them, and put them into a casserole, together with a clove of garlic and a bay leaf. Cover with cold water, bring to the boil, and then turn down the heat to its lowest setting. Cover the pan, and simmer slowly for about two and a half hours. Only add salt towards the end of this time. Wash the clams under running water, and leave them in water until it is time to cook them. When the beans are nearly ready, put some olive oil in a large frying pan, and brown the whole crushed garlic cloves. Add the clams and plenty of pepper. Cover the pan and keep it on a high heat for a few minutes to open up the shells. Take up the clams with a strainer, shell them and discard any that are still closed. Keep about twenty with their shells on for decoration. Add the contents of the frying pan to the casserole containing the beans using a fine-meshed sieve to keep back any possible grains of sand. Add the clams and the pasta, mix together, and cook for about a quarter of an hour, adding salt if necessary.

When the pasta is cooked, discard the garlic cloves and let everything cool a little for a few minutes before serving.

Pasta agli sconcigli / Pasta with shellfish

300 g (10 oz) spaghetti
800 g (2 pounds) shellfish
2 shallots
parsley
dry white wine
1 chilli
half a lemon
400 g (14 oz) peeled tomatoes
extra virgin olive oil, salt

Wash the shellfish very thoroughly, and scald them for half an hour in lightly salted water acidulated with the juice of half a lemon. As soon as the water has cooled to lukewarm, take the molluscs out of their shells and remove the hard membranes. Cut up the molluscs really finely, and brown them in the olive oil together with the shallots, chilli and parsley which have first been pounded together.

Add the white wine, let it evaporate and then add the finely chopped tomatoes. Salt lightly and continue cooking for 15 minutes. Meanwhile, cook the spaghetti until still fairly firm (al dente), and then add the shellfish sauce.

Sprinkle with chopped fresh parsley before serving.

300 g (10 oz) linguine pasta
500 g (1 pound) real clams
4 medium sized corgettes
½ glass extra virgin olive oil
1 shallot
1 clove garlic
parsley
salt and pepper

Rinse the clams very thoroughly and put them in plenty of salted water for several hours to get rid of the sand. Clean the corgettes and slice them thinly. Finely chop the shallots. Pour half of the olive oil into a baking pan and put in the corgettes and chopped shallots. Mix them together, and salt them lightly. Put the pan into the pre-heated oven, and cook for about 20 minutes at 180 C. (390 F.), until the corgettes are cooked.

In the meantime, heat up the rest of the oil in a frying pan, and brown the peeled and crushed garlic clove.

Add the drained clams, cover, and shake the pan lightly, leaving it on the heat until all the shellfish are open. Add the corgettes and the chopped parsley and let the flavours mingle for a few minutes.

Cook the pasta in salted water, drain whilst still quite firm (al dente), and toss in the frying pan containing the clams and corgettes to mix it all together.

Serve very hot with a sprinkling of pepper.

Giuseppe Recco, *Fish,* Florence, Pitti Palace (in storage)

Cacciucco / Fish chowder

1500 g (3 pounds) of assorted
fish (red mullet, octopus,
scorpion fish, cuttlefish, hake,
mussels, squill fish, squid,
conger, dogfish, mantis shrimps,
crab)
100 g (3 ½ oz) extra virgin olive
oil
2 onions, 2 carrots, 2 sticks of
celery
1 kg (2 pounds) peeled tomatoes
3 cloves of garlic, parsley
2 tablespoons vinegar
chilli
red wine
home-made bread
salt

Clean the fish: with suitable scissors remove the fins and heads, reserving the latter to make stock. Rinse the fish under running water, and prepare it for cooking. Cut the larger fish into slices so that all the fish need the same cooking time. Use a small hard brush to clean the mussels under a jet of water, and if necessary scrape them with a knife. Skin the soft body "bag" part of the cuttlefish and octopus, wash them, dry them on kitchen paper and cut them into strips. Wash and dry the tentacles and cut them up very small.

Put the fish heads and scraps, previously set aside, into a stock pot and cover them with cold water. Add a stick of celery, a carrot and an onion, all cleaned and chopped, plus parsley tied into a bunch, a clove of garlic, and salt to taste. Cover, bring to the boil, then turn the heat down to a minimum and simmer for three quarters of an hour.

Chop the peeled tomatoes. Heat up the oil in a large saucepan, and over a moderate heat brown an onion, a carrot and a celery stick, all chopped. Wash some parsley and finely chop it, together with two peeled cloves of garlic and the chilli. When the onion in the pan starts to turn colour, add the garlic, parsley and chilli mixture, and let fit all sizzle a moment before adding the strips of cuttlefish and octopus. Turn up the heat, add salt, and let the pan contents dry out, stirring frequently. When the fish start to turn

a golden colour, moisten with the vinegar, and as soon as this has evaporated, add the wine and then the tomatoes immediately afterwards. Cover, and continue cooking until the cuttlefish and octopus are tender and the sauce has been reduced to the right consistency.

In the meantime, the fish stock will be ready. Retrieve and set aside the little bits of fish flesh which will have separated out. Pass everything else through a vegetable sieve, using the finest disc, paying special attention to the fish heads and bones which will make the sauce thicker and give it more flavour. Add this sauce to the one with the octopus and tomatoes, and then add the little pieces of fish previously set aside, and bring everything to the boil. Put the mussels into a frying pan, cover it, and keep it on a high heat until all the mussel shells are open. Discard the opened shell halves, and add the liquid which came out of them to the fish sauce, passing it through a fine strainer lined with kitchen paper. Season with salt to taste, and then add the fish, starting with the toughest (mantis shrimps, conger and dogfish), followed by scorpion fish and lastly add the crab and the mussels. Cook all the fish together for not more than about a quarter of an hour in all. Toast the bread slices, rub them lightly with a clove of garlic, put them in a soup tureen and pour in the fish chowder.

Cestini con polpettine di gamberoni / Little pastry baskets with crayfish rissoles

125 g (4 ½ oz) roll of frozen flaky
pastry
3 spring onions
100 g (3 ½ oz) minced pork
100 g (3 ½ oz) shelled crayfish
garlic, onion, celery, carrot
1 egg white
parsley
extra virgin olive oil
salt, chilli

Thaw the pastry at room temperature, then unroll it and flatten it out more with a rolling pin to a thickness of 1 millimetre. Use a suitable little wheeled gadget to make a basket pattern. Cut out from the pastry four squares with sides of 12 cm, and mould each one by hand round the reverse side of little tartlet tins and put these in the oven for five minutes at 200 C. (390 F.). Cool the baking tins, and then very carefully take off the little pastry baskets which have been made in this way.

Put three tablespoonfuls of oil in a pan and lightly fry half a garlic clove, a piece of onion, a small carrot and a small stick of celery, all very finely minced.

Process together the meat, crayfish, spring onions, minced fried vegetables, the chilli and a pinch of salt. Blend in the egg white and then by hand form little nut-sized rissoles. Fry these in boiling oil, and drain on absorbent kitchen paper. Divide up the rissoles between the pastry baskets, and decorate with a crayfish and a few parsley leaves before serving.

Pane di tonno / Tuna fish bread

300 g (10 oz) tinned tuna fish,
in water
100 g (3 ½ oz) parmesan
100 g + 1 tablespoon (3 ½ oz and
a tablespoon) flour
3 eggs
7 tablespoons milk
3 tablespoons extra virgin olive
oil
1 packet pizza yeast
20 g (1 oz) butter
salt and white pepper

Drain and mince the fish. Put the flour in a bowl, add the eggs and beat the mixture until smooth. Add the milk and oil. Heat the oven to 200 C. (390 F.). Add the yeast, tuna fish and cheese to the mixture, and season with salt and pepper. Put the mixture, into a floured and buttered cake tin, and bake in the oven for 40 minutes.

Giacomo Fardella, *Fish,* Florence, Pitti Palace (in storage)

Spaghetti con aragosta / Spaghetti with lobster

300 g (10 oz) spaghetti
1 lobster (feminine) weighing
700 - 800 g (2 pounds)
½ red onion
200 g (7 oz) peeled tomatoes
marjoram

Open up the lobster and cut it into pieces. Scald it in boiling water for five minutes and extract all the pulp. Brown the chopped half onion together with an unpeeled garlic clove.

When the garlic has turned colour, take it out of the pan and add the pieces of lobster, the peeled tomatoes and lastly the marjoram. Cook all this until the lobster is tender. Separately, cook the spaghetti until still fairly firm (al dente), and then toss it in the pan with the prepared sauce.

Salmone sul sale / Salmon on salt

1 salmon weighing about 1 kg
(2 pounds)
butter
thyme
lemon
dry white wine
onion
coarse and fine salt

Marinade the cleaned salmon for at least three hours in the wine plus several slices of lemon. Prepare a baking pan by covering the base with coarsely ground salt. Drain the salmon, salt and pepper it on the inside, and fill it up, lengthways along the slit, with onion rings, lemon slices, pieces of butter and fresh or dried thyme. Place the fish on top of the coarse salt, and put the pan in a moderate oven. Whilst it is cooking, baste the fish with the wine used for the marinade.

Untie and serve the salmon with mayonnaise to which has been added a small glass of yoghurt, a tablespoonful of water and minced pickled gherkins, or simply serve it with very hot melted butter, accompanied by steamed vegetables.

Ravioli di pesce / Fish ravioli

For the pasta:
300 g (10 oz) flour
2 eggs
1 tablespoon extra virgin olive oil
salt

For the filling:
500 g (1 pound) sole (or white
bream or scorpion fish)
400 g (1 pound) endives
100 g (3 ½ oz) ricotta from
sheep's milk
1 egg
2 tablespoons grated parmesan
1 tablespoon extra virgin olive oil
marjoram, 1 clove garlic
salt and pepper

For the sauce:
800 g (2 pounds) mussels with
their shells
200 g (7 oz) tomato pulp
1/2 glass dry white wine
2 tablespoons extra virgin olive oil
parsley, salt and pepper

Scale and clean the fish and sort out two to four fillets. Make sure that all the bones have been properly removed, then rinse and dry the fillets using kitchen paper. Heat up the oil in a non-stick frying pan, and over a moderate heat brown the lightly crushed garlic clove. Put the fish fillets in to the pan, season with salt and pepper, and let them brown on both sides for a few minutes, then break them up in a bowl, using a fork.

Clean the endives, removing the toughest and damaged leaves, then strip off the other leaves, wash them well and scald for three or four minutes in boiling salted water. Drain the leaves, let them cool a little, and squeeze them out well in a cloth. Chop them very finely indeed and add to the fish. Now add the ricotta as well, plus the grated parmesan, the whole egg, a pinch of marjoram and a pinch of salt. Blend it all well together, cover, and keep it on one side.

To prepare the pasta, sieve the flour on to the pastry board, make a well in the centre, and tip in the beaten egg, a pinch of salt, a tablespoonful of oil and a little tepid water. Blend, and work it vigorously with the hands for about ten minutes until the dough has smooth elastic texture. Cover with a cloth, and let it rest for half an hour. Meanwhile, prepare the sauce. Remove the barbels from the mussels, then scrub the latter with a hard brush under a jet of water. Put the cleaned mussels in a pan on the stove to open all the valves of the shells. Drain them, reserving the liquid which came out of the mussels, then shell and mince them. Add two tablespoonfuls of oil and brown the shellfish. Stir them, and as soon as they start to dry out, pour on the wine. Let this reduce, add the tomato pulp and the liquid which came out of the mussels, pouring it through a fine sieve to hold back any possible grains of sand. Season with salt and pepper to taste, and cook it all over a high heat for ten minutes. Divide the pasta dough into three pieces and roll each one out into a thin strip. Put cherry-sized mounds of the filling lengthways along the strip of pasta, about 4 cm apart from each other. Fold over the pasta dough on top of the little mounds and use fingers to press firmly down round each bit of filling to eliminate any air and to seal it well. Use the little notched-wheel gadget (i.e. a pastry cutter) to cut out the filled ravioli shapes and then put these on to a floured cloth.

When they are all ready, plunge them in boiling salted water to cook them for about 7 - 8 minutes. Drain with a slotted spoon, put the ravioli on a serving dish and dress with the very hot sauce. Sprinkle with chopped parsley and serve immediately.

Giuseppe Maria Crespi, *Fish,* Florence, Uffizi Gallery (in storage)

Calamari ripieni al prosciutto / Cuttlefish with a ham stuffing

4 cuttlefish, each weighing about
200 g (7 oz)
100 g (3 ½ oz) smoked ham
3 ripe tomatoes
1 large onion
2 cloves garlic
parsley
salt, pepper
extra virgin olive oil

Clean and gut the cuttlefish, cut off the tentacles and mince them together with the ham, adding salt, pepper and chopped parsley. Blend well to make a smooth mixture and use this to stuff the cuttlefish three-quarters full. Close up the sides with a toothpick. Heat up a few tablespoonfuls of oil over a low heat and gently fry the finely chopped onion and the whole cloves of garlic. When the onion has softened, remove the garlic, put in the cuttlefish and continue cooking them for 20 minutes, adding white wine and the finely chopped tomatoes. If the sauce is too thin towards the end of the cooking time, it can be thickened by the addition of a nut of butter mixed with flour. Serve the fish sprinkled with chopped parsley.

Alici al pomodoro / Anchovies with tomatoes

800 g (2 pounds) fresh anchovies
300 g (10 oz) tomato pulp
2 tablespoons extra virgin olive
oil
1 clove garlic
parsley, marjoram, salt and
pepper

Bone and gut the anchovies and remove the heads leaving the rest of the fish intact. Wash them under running water, then dry them. Peel the clove of garlic, removing its little core, and then mince the garlic very finely together with a small bunch of parsley and a pinch of marjoram. Cover the base of a round oven dish with half the tomato pulp, and put the anchovies on top of this. Season with salt and pepper, and sprinkle with the garlic-parsley mixture. Add the remaining tomato pulp and the oil, put the dish into the oven, pre-heated to 180 C. (350 F.) and cook the contents for 15 minutes. Let the anchovies cool off slightly before serving them, sprinkled with fresh parsley.

Pasta con le sarde / Pasta with sardines

500 g (1 pound) bucatini or
   spaghetti
500 g (1 pound) fresh sardines
6 sprigs of wild fennel
3 anchovies in salt
1 medium onion
1 tablespoon sultanas
1 tablespoon pine kernels
1 tablespoon finely chopped
roasted almonds
1 tablespoon—tip of saffron
4 tablespoons of extra virgin olive oil
salt and pepper

Wash and bone the anchovies. Soak the sultanas in a cup of lukewarm water. Clean the fennel and retain only the tender bits. Rinse the fennel and boil it for 15 minutes in salted water. When it is cooked, take it out with a slotted spoon, and keep the water to use for cooking the pasta. Whilst the fennel is cooking, wash and dry the sardines, first scraping away the scales and removing the heads and bones.

Take a non-stick frying pan, large enough to toss the pasta, heat up half the oil and quickly turn the sardines in it. Take them out of the pan and put them aside. Slice the onion very thinly and put it in the pan to brown. When it has slightly turned colour, add the chopped fennel, the pine kernels, the drained and dried sultanas and the seared sardines. Season with salt and pepper to taste, and continue cooking, stirring occasionally with a wooden spoon. The fish should disintegrate and blend into the sauce. In the meantime, break up the prepared anchovy fillets mixing them with the rest of the oil, and add them to the sardines and fennel, then continue cooking them for 30 minutes in all.

Towards the end, add the saffron which has been dissolved in a tablespoonful of water. Cook the bucatini pasta in the water used for cooking the fennel, previously put aside, and then toss the cooked pasta in the frying pan together with the prepared sauce. Sprinkle with chopped almonds.

Jan van Kessel, *Fish on the seashore,* Florence, Pitti Palace, Palatine Gallery

Spaghetti alla razza / Spaghetti with rayfish

400 g (1 pound) spaghetti
800 g (2 pounds) ripe tomatoes
400 g (1 pound) skinned rayfish
3 tablespoons extra virgin olive oil
2 cloves garlic
parsley, salt

Plunge the tomatoes in boiling water for 30 seconds, then put them into cold water, peel them, remove the seeds and cut the tomatoes up small. Put them into a frying pan with the olive oil, plus the finely chopped garlic and parsley. Put the pan on the stove and cook the contents for about 10 minutes. Add the rayfish, cut into four or five pieces. Season with salt, and cook over a high heat for a further 10 minutes until the sauce is reduced. Take out the pieces of rayfish, remove the cartilage and put the filleted fish flesh back into the sauce.

Bring it all back to the boil, and serve the sauce as a flavoursome accompaniment to the spaghetti which are cooked but still firm (al dente)

Pasta e broccoli in brodo di razza / Pasta and broccoli in a rayfish broth

1 kg (2 pounds) rayfish
500 g (1 pound) broccoli
200 g (7 oz) of fine pasta, or broken-up spaghetti
200 g (7 oz) peeled tomatoes
1 anchovy in salt
2 tablespoons extra virgin olive oil
1 onion, 1 carrot
1 stick of celery
1 clove garlic
parsley, chilli
½ glass white wine
salt

Wash the fish under running water, and put it in a saucepan with about one and a half litres of cold water. Season with salt, and add the celery, carrot, onion and parsley, all of them finely chopped. Cover, and simmer on a very low heat for 20 minutes. When the fish is cooked, take it out of the water with a slotted spoon, and trim and prepare it by removing the head, skin and cartilage. Set aside the resulting filleted fish flesh, and put all the scraps back into the pan containing the stock, and continue cooking this for a further half hour. In the meantime, pound together the garlic clove, a handful of parsley and a little chilli and soften this mixture in a saucepan containing the olive oil.

Add the boned and cleaned anchovy, crushing it with a fork, then add the chopped tomatoes and the wine, cover the saucepan, and cook the contents over a moderate heat for 20 minutes.

Divide the broccoli into little pieces, wash, and add these to the sauce, letting the flavours mingle for a few minutes, with the saucepan lid off. Pour the stock through a sieve directly into the saucepan containing the broccoli, stir it in, cover, and continue cooking for ten minutes.

Mix in the pasta, and cook it all together for about 15 minutes. Serve the broth very hot.

Bartolomeo Bimbi, *Apples,* Poggio a Caiano, Villa Medicea Florence, Florentine galleries (in storage)

Anatra alle mele / Duck with apples

1 young duck weighing approx.
1 kg. 200 g (2 ½ pounds)
2 "rennet" apples
30 g (1 oz) butter
1 glass dry white wine
1 small glass Calvados
3 tablespoons cream, tarragon,
salt

Clean the duck. Singe it carefully to eliminate the down and use pincers to take out any spiky ends of feathers left in the skin. Remove all fatty deposits from inside the bird, then wash and dry it, and season with salt both inside and out. Put a few sprigs of fresh tarragon (or a pinch of dried) inside the cavity, and tie up the duck to keep it in shape. Put it in a pan with half of the butter, and brown it evenly on all sides over a high heat, turning it frequently. When the bird is a good colour, discard all the fat and pour in the Calvados. Let this reduce, then cover the pan and continue cooking the duck for 45 minutes over a moderate heat, turning it three or four times and moistening it as necessary with a few tablespoonfuls of hot water.

Peel the apples, cut them into eight segments and let them brown for ten minutes in a frying pan with a little butter. When the duck is cooked, put it out on a plate and keep it warm in a lukewarm oven. Pour the wine into the pan and reduce it by half over a high heat, stirring with a wooden spoon to take up the cooking sediment. Add a few leaves of tarragon and the cream, simmer for a few minutes and then pour the sauce into a gravy boat.

Arrange the duck on a serving dish, surrounded by the apple slices, and serve hot with the sauce as accompaniment.

Torta di mele e more / Apple and blackberry tart

250 g (1/2 pound) wholemeal flour
125 g (5 oz) butter
40 g (4 tablespoons) sugar
6 "Granny Smith" apples
450 g (1 pound) blackberries
2 tablespoons sugar
1 tablespoon wholemeal flour
fresh cream

Put the flour, cubed butter and 40 g of sugar into the blender to make a crumbly mixture. Add two tablespoons of chilled water and blend again to make a pastry dough. Roll it out into a circle 30 - 35 cm in diameter, and put it into a baking tin 24 cm in diameter, previously lined with oven-proof paper.

Mix together in a bowl the peeled and thinly sliced apples, the blackberries and two tablespoonfuls of sugar, plus one tablespoonful of wholemeal flour. Put all this into the pastry-lined tin, and bake in a hot oven at 200 C. (390 F.) for 35 minutes. Serve the tart lukewarm with lightly whipped cream.

Gratin di pere e mandorle / Baked pears and almonds

2 small William pears
100 g (3 ½ oz) acacia honey
100 g (3 ½ oz) sugar
1 vanilla pod
1 stick of cinnamon
500 g (1 pound) almonds, ground powder-fine
30 g (1 oz) almonds
50 g (2 oz) butter
1 egg
clove powder

Wash the pears and remove the stalks, then cut the pears in half, and take out the cores. Take a small saucepan, and put in the sugar, 3 dl of water, the cinnamon and the vanilla, and bring it all to the boil. Add the pears and simmer them slowly for five minutes, on a very low heat.
Separately, melt the butter in a small pan. Meanwhile, break the egg into a bowl, and stir in the ground almonds, the honey, the

melted butter and clove powder. Divide this mixture between four individual heat-resistant glass bowls, strain the pears out of the syrup, and put half a pear in the middle of each bowl. Sprinkle them with flakes of almond and the remaining sugar. Bake them for 10 minutes in the oven, pre-heated to 200 C.(390 F.)
Serve hot or lukewarm.

Cristoforo Munari, *Fruit and musical instruments,* Roma, Montecitorio Palace, the Parliament
Florentine galleries (in storage)

Arrosto di maiale con le mele / Roast pork with apples

800 g (2 pounds) loin of pork
2 large dessert apples
2 tablespoons extra virgin olive oil
15 g (1 tablespoon) butter
½ glass dry white wine
2 cloves
2 bay leaves
cinnamon powder
salt and pepper

Crush the cloves and mix them with a finely chopped bay leaf, a grinding of pepper and a pinch of cinnamon. Sprinkle this mixture over the meat, then put the meat in a dish, cover it, and leave it overnight in the fridge to absorb the flavours. Before cooking it, take it out of the marinade, and tie it up to keep its shape. Put the oil and butter into a heavy-based pan, add a bay leaf, and add the meat when the fat starts to sputter. Brown it all over on a moderate heat, turning it frequently without piercing it. When the meat is well browned, add the wine, let it reduce, season with salt, cover the pan and continue cooking on a moderate heat for about an hour, turning the meat occasionally. If the meat is inclined to stick to the pan, add a few spoonfuls of stock or water. Peel and core the apples and cut them up into eight pieces. Put them into the pan and after they have been cooking for 40 minutes, turn up the heat and stir them so that they are well flavoured, then lower the heat again for the rest of the cooking time. As they disintegrate, the apples produce plenty of sauce. Just before serving, untie the meat, slice it thinly and arrange it on a serving dish covered with the hot apple sauce.

Gelo di cocomero / Water melon jelly

1 kg (2 pounds) well-ripened
water melon flesh, without seeds
200 g (7 oz) sugar
90 g (3 oz) corn flour
50 g (2 oz) candied pumpkin, in
little cubes
50 g (2 oz) plain dark chocolate,
in little bits
30 g (1 oz) pistachio nuts
1 stick of cinnamon
powdered cinnamon
a pinch of vanilla

Scald the pistachio nuts in boiling water for a few minutes then shell them. Use a finely meshed sieve or vegetable mill to sieve the water melon pulp into a heavy based steel saucepan. Put some of the juice obtained into a cup and dissolve the corn flour in it to make a fine paste without any lumps. Pour this back into the pan also adding the sugar and the stick of cinnamon. Mix well, put the pan on the stove, and bring its contents to the boil, stirring continuously. Continue cooking on a moderate heat for four or five minutes, stirring all the time.

Take the pan off the heat, and as soon as the mixture starts to cool and thicken, remove the cinnamon stick and add the chocolate bits, the vanilla, the candied pumpkin and the pistachio nuts. Either put it all into one fluted mould, or divide it between individual moulds, rinsed out with water. Let it rest in the fridge for several hours, or overnight.
Just before serving the jelly, turn it out on to a plate, and sprinkle with powdered cinnamon.
Decorate with lemon and jasmine leaves.

Tagliolini al limone / Tagliolini pasta with lemon

400 g (1 pound) fresh tagliolini
pasta
1 tablespoon butter
1 lemon
½ glass white wine
½ cup cream
white pepper, salt
4 tablespoons grated parmesan

Cook the pasta for one minute in boiling water.
Meanwhile, melt half the butter in a frying pan and grate the lemon peel into it. Pour in half a glass of white wine, let it evaporate and simmer very briefly. Add the cream and

a shake of white pepper.
Drain the pasta and toss it in the pan with the sauce. Flavour it with the grated cheese, the juice of half a lemon, and the remaining butter.

Abraham Mignon, *Table with fruit and objects,* Florence, Uffizi Gallery

Crostata di limone / Lemon tart

For the pastry:
200 g (7 oz) flour
125 g (5 oz) butter
a little extra butter to grease the
baking tin
100 g (4 oz) sugar
1 egg
1 lemon

For the filling:
2 very juicy lemons
100 g (4 oz) butter
100 g (4 oz) sugar
3 eggs
200 g (7 oz) wild strawberries
or raspberries

First make the pastry. Wash the lemons and grate the zest into a bowl (only the yellow part of the peel).

Add the diced and softened butter, plus the sugar, and work it all together with a wooden spoon for about ten minutes until the mixture is smooth and light. Add the whole egg, blend it in, then add the sieved flour, and continue working it all together rapidly, with the fingertips, until the pastry has a smooth consistency.

Make a ball of the pastry dough, wrap it up in a cloth and let it rest in the least cold part of the fridge for several hours (or even overnight).

To make the lemon cream filling, wash and dry the lemons, and finely grate the yellow outside zest into a little bowl. Squeeze the lemons (including the one used for the pastry), and pour 200 g (1/2 cup) of the juice into the bowl with the grated zest. Put the butter into a heavy-based pan, and put this pan into another slightly larger pan which is three quarters full of extremely hot, but not boiling water. When the butter has melted, add the sugar and then, stirring continually, add the separately beaten eggs, plus the lemon juice and grated rind. Continue stirring and cook all this for five minutes until the lemon cream has thickened. Sieve it, cover it, and allow to cool.

Butter a baking tin, 26 cm in diameter, and line it with the pastry, rolled out about ½ cm thick, and remove any surplus pastry. Prick the pastry base all over with a fork and then cover it with a sheet of oven paper, and fill this with dried beans. Put the tin in the oven, pre-heated to 180 C. (350 F.) and blind bake the pastry for about 10 minutes. At the end of this time, remove the oven paper and the dried beans, and put the pastry case back in the oven for a further quarter of an hour, then take it out and let it get cold. Fill it with the lemon cream and put it in the fridge for at least an hour.

Just before serving, decorate the tart with little strawberries or raspberries.

Bartolomeo Bimbi, *Citrus fruit,* Poggio a Caiano, Villa Medicea, Florentine galleries (in storage)

Scorzette di arancia al cioccolato / Orange peel with chocolate

2 or 3 oranges
sugar
plain chocolate

Peel the oranges, discarding all the white pith. Soak the peel in cold water for three days, changing the water twice a day. At the end of this time, boil the peel in half a litre of water for 15 minutes, then drain it and cut it into little strips. Weigh the strips of peel, then add an equal weight of sugar and just enough water to dissolve it. Cook it all together until the sugar turns white as it dries round the peel. Turn the peel out on to a cloth, keeping the pieces well separated from each other. When cold, dip the pieces of peel, one at a time, into the melted chocolate (which should not be too hot), and then spread them out on aluminium foil. Serve cold.

These strips of chocolate peel will keep if stored in an airtight tin, in a cool place.

A speedier method is to use pieces of candied orange peel to dip into the chocolate.

Limoncello / Lemon liqueur

½ litre (2 cups) of pure alcohol 90°
Unsprayed lemons - 5 or 6, according to size
500 g (1 pound) sugar
½ litre (2 cups) water

Thinly peel the lemons with a potato peeler, only removing the yellow outside part. Put this outer peel, together with the alcohol, into a hermetically sealed jar and leave to infuse in a cool dry place for 24 days. At the end of this time, prepare a syrup by boiling together 500 g (1 pound) sugar in half a litre (2 cups) of water, for five minutes. Let it cool completely. Pour the lemon-flavoured alcohol and lemon peel through a strainer into the cold syrup. Sieve once more, and then bottle.

Wait a few weeks before using.

Sorbetto al mandarino / Mandarin orange sorbet

8 mandarins
450 g (1 pound) fresh mandarin juice
1 lemon, 1 egg white
100 g (4 oz) sugar

Cut off the tops and hollow out six mandarins, putting the empty shells aside for later. To the mandarin juice obtained, add the juice of one lemon. Put 200 g (1 cup) of water in a pan on the stove, together with the sugar and the grated zest of two mandarins. Let it boil whilst stirring for a few minutes and then allow to cool. Strain the syrup and add the lemon and mandarin juice, passed through a fine sieve. Carefully fold in the stiffly-beaten egg white, and put the mixture into the ice cream machine. When the sorbet is ready, fill it into the empty mandarin shells which were put aside.

Keep them in the freezer until it is time to serve them.

Bartolomeo Bimbi, *Dates,* Florence, Pitti Palace (in storage)

Insalata di riso e datteri / Rice and date salad

250 g (8 oz) Carnaroli rice
1 head of endive salad
2 tablespoons nut kernels
20 dates
2 small carrots, salt
extra virgin olive oil

Boil the rice in lightly salted water, and cook it just enough so that the grains of rice are still well separated. Spoon the rice into small transparent individual bowls. Season it with a drizzle of olive oil and salt if necessary. Carefully cut the dates into small pieces and insert three or four cut-up dates into the rice in each bowl. Sprinkle with the finely ground nut kernels, and then cover the rice with very fine strips of chicory, and garnish it all with a date.

Cut the carrots into minute squares, and arrange these at one side of the bowls to give a bit of colour. The salad can now be served. People at the table will have to toss their own rice salad, possibly adding some of the olive oil which is served separately.

Biscottini con i datteri / Little date biscuits

300 g (10 oz) sugar
4 tablespoons honey
400 g (1 pound) semolina
100 g (3 ½ oz) couscous
1 generous pinch baking soda
1 pinch curcuma
scant ½ tablespoon salt
1 dl (5 tablespoons) extra virgin olive oil
250 g (8 oz) soft dates
1 orange
powdered cinnamon
oil for frying

Prepare a syrup by dissolving the sugar in half a litre of water in a pan on the stove. Bring it to the boil, and simmer for 2 - 3 minutes. Add the honey, and as soon as this has melted, take it all off the stove. Mix together the semolina, couscous, baking soda and curcuma, and make a well of this mixture on the work table. Pour in 60 g (3 tbs) of lukewarm olive oil, and a generous 2 dl (1 cup) of water, a little at a time, working the mixture so as to make a smooth, even and fairly firm dough. Let it rest for half an hour. Meanwhile, stone the dates and chop them very finely. Add the grated rind of half an orange, two pinches of cinnamon, plus two tablespoonfuls of oil, and work the mixture to form three cylindrical shapes. Put these aside. When the pastry dough has rested enough, divide this into three pieces. Roll each one into a rectangle, 1 cm thick, a little longer than the date mixture cylinders. Put the date mixture in the centre of the pastry rectangles, fold them over at the edges and then roll them up to form a cylinder. Flatten the cylinders with a rolling pin to a thickness of about 1 cm, and cut out little diamond shapes about 2 - 3 cm wide. Grease each one with oil before frying. Heat up the syrup, fry the biscuits in plenty of oil, drain, and throw them in the hot syrup, little by little, as they are ready. Drain them after they have been soaking in the syrup for ten minutes. Serve lukewarm or cold.

Bartolomeo Ligozzi, *Fruit and flowers,* Florence, Pitti Palace (in storage)

Pere giugnoline / June pears

500 g (1 pound) June pears
200 g (7 oz) mild gorgonzola
cheese
or 200 g (7 oz) gorgonzola and
mascarpone mixed
1 lemon

Core the pears and dip them into lemon juice to prevent them turning black, then fill the hollows left from the cores with a lightly whipped mixture of gorgonzola and mascarpone, or else sweet mascarpone lightly whipped up with a fork. Serve as an appetizer.

Datteri ripieni al sorbetto di pere / Stuffed dates with pear sorbet

500 g (1 pound) pear sorbet
3 unsprayed clementines, with
a few leaves
1 dl (1 small glass) vodka
8 fresh dates
80 g (3 oz) shelled pistachio nuts
40 g (1 ½ oz) shelled almonds
30 g (1 oz) icing sugar
½ tablespoon cinnamon
clove powder
nutmeg
orange flower water
castor sugar

Put the shelled and peeled almonds into a small non-stick frying pan, and brown them over a low heat. Scald the pistachio nuts in boiling water for two minutes, then drain and peel them. Blend together in the mixer the pistachio nuts and almonds, adding a few drops of orange flower water, a pinch of nutmeg, the cinnamon and the icing sugar, processing them together to make a smooth paste.

Peel the dates, slit them lengthways, remove the stones and stuff them with a little ball of the pistachio and almond paste. Close the opening, and dust the dates with icing sugar. Wash the clementines, slice them very thinly without peeling them, and line a large transparent dessert bowl. Arrange the washed and dried clementine leaves, and put the sorbet (which should not be frozen too hard) into the middle of the bowl. Pour the vodka over the sorbet, dust with a pinch of clove-flavoured pepper, and serve with the stuffed dates.

Giovanni Pini, *Landscape with still life of fruit,* Florence, Pitti Palace (in storage)

Cotognata / Quince jelly

1 kg (2 pound) quinces
1 kg and 300 g (3 pounds) sugar
2 lemons
½ glass water

Core and peel the quinces, then put them into water acidulated with the juice of 1 ½ lemons to prevent them turning black. Put the quinces into a pan together with half a glass of water and the juice and peel (without pith) of half a lemon. Bring to the boil whilst stirring. When the quinces are cooked, rub them through a sieve. Put them back into the pan with the sugar and boil again, stirring constantly and skimming off the froth until the mixture is firm and has a smooth appearance. Put it into a shallow container whilst still hot and sprinkle with sugar. It should be spread about 1 ½ to 2 cm thick.

When the quince jelly is cold, it can be cut into little squares, dipped in sugar and kept in a closed tin in a dry place.

Marmellata di mele cotogne / Quince jam

1 kg (2 pounds) quinces
sugar as necessary
1 lemon
alcohol 95°

Choose very sound ripe quinces, wash them under running water, put them in a pan covered with cold water, and cook them until the skins start to split.

Weigh a stainless steel preserving pan, big enough to take both quinces and sugar. Drain the quinces, let them cool a little, and then peel them. Cut them into little bits and rub them through a fine-meshed sieve into the previously weighed pan. Calculate the weight of the fruit by subtracting the weight of the pan from the total weight of the pan plus fruit. Add an amount of sugar equal to the weight of the fruit. Mix together and cook on a moderate heat for about an hour and a half. The jam is ready when a small drop on a sloping plate stays firm and set without sliding off the plate. Take the pan off the stove and flavour the jam with a few drops of lemon juice mixing well. Fill it into jars whilst still hot to within 2 cm of the brim. Cover the jars with a table napkin, put a cloth on top of this, and leave the jam to get cold until the following day. Cut out little rounds of oiled paper, dip them into 95° alcohol, and place them on top of the jam. Close the jars with an airtight seal, and keep them in a cool dark airy place.

Bartolomeo Bimbi, *Pears,* Poggio a Caiano, Villa Medicea, Florentine galleries (in storage)

Pere al vino rosso / Pears in red wine

4 "Kaiser" pears
lemon peel
red wine

Keep the pears at room temperature for several days so that they are not too firm and have flavour. After this, cook the whole peeled pears in red wine and sugar plus a few little bits of cinnamon and lemon peel. Let the pears cool in their cooking liquid, and serve them with cream.

Tortino di pere / Pears in batter tart

4 or 5 "Kaiser" pears
250 g (1 cup) milk
2 eggs
80 g (2 ½ oz) flour
1 tablespoon sugar
15 g (1 tablespoon) butter
1 tablespoon vanilla sugar

Peel and core the pears and cut them into segments. Put the whole eggs, flour, sugar and milk into a bowl and use the electric mixer to work them into a smooth batter. Generously butter and flour an oven dish, 24 cm in diameter, and arrange the pear segments inside it in tightly packed circle form, and then pour in the prepared batter. Put the dish into the oven, pre-heated to 180 C. (350 F.) and bake the mixture for 50 minutes. When cooked, take the dessert out of the oven and sprinkle with icing sugar. Serve lukewarm directly out of the oven dish.

Sorbetto di pere / Pear sorbet

800 g (2 pounds) ripe "William"
pears
250 g (10 oz) sugar
1 lemon
1 egg white
pear liqueur

Make a syrup by boiling 250 g (1 cup) of water with an equal amount of sugar. Peel and core the pears, quickly rub them through a sieve and mix them with the juice of a large lemon. Add the fruit puree to the cold syrup, and carefully fold in the stiffly beaten egg white. Put the mixture in the ice-cream machine.

When the sorbet has been distributed into little dessert bowls, add a few spoonfuls of a good quality pear liqueur as a finishing touch.

Giovanna Garzoni, *Fruit dish of plums with pears and cherries,* Florence, Uffizi Gallery,
Print and and drawing cabinet

Gratin di patate e pere / Baked potatoes and pears

2 small "decana" pears
3 potatoes
50 g (4 tablespoons) parmesan
milk
40 g (1 ½ oz)butter
salt, freshly ground pepper

Peel and slice the potatoes. Peel and core the pears and slice them to the same thickness as the potato slices. Season both pears and potatoes with salt and pepper.
Butter an oven proof dish and arrange the pear and potato slices in alternate layers. Sprinkle with parmesan. When the dish is full, pour in the milk to cover the potatoes and pears, dot with butter, and bake in a pre-heated oven at 200 C. (390 F.) for 45 minutes.

Crostata di susine gialle / Yellow plum tart

For the short crust pastry:
200 g (8 oz) flour
100 g (4 oz) butter
80 g (3 oz) sugar
1 egg yolk
1 packet vanilla
pinch of salt

For the filling:
200 g (8 oz) plum jam
5 yellow plums
30 g (1 oz) almond chips
2 tablespoons sugar

Put the butter and the sugar into a bowl, cream them together and add the vanilla, salt, and the egg yolk. Sieve in the flour, and work it all into a pastry dough. Cover with transparent cellophane and let it rest in the fridge for about an hour. At the end of this time, butter and flour a tart tin, line both base and sides with the pastry, and prick it with a fork. Spoon the jam on top of the pastry and level it off.
Wash and dry the plums, cut them in half and remove the stones, then arrange the halved plums on top of the jam, cut side up. Sprinkle with sugar and scatter with the almond chips. Put the tart in the oven, pre-heated to 180°C. (350 F.) for about 40 minutes. Turn it out of the tin and let it cool.

*T*ortine di mele e pere / *P*ear and apple tartlets

100 g (4 oz) flour
50 g (2 oz) bran flour
2 tablespoons extra virgin olive oil
1 tablespoon acacia honey
50 g (1/4 cup) apple juice
1 unsprayed orange
2 pears
10 g (1 tablespoon) butter
1 tablespoon cane sugar
2 cloves
2 apples
icing sugar
yeast
Calvados
salt and pepper

On a floured pastry board, make the pastry by quickly working together the two kinds of flour, the oil, honey, the grated rind of half an orange, the apple juice, a pinch of yeast and a pinch of salt. Form it into a ball of dough, wrap it up in a clean cloth and put it in the fridge for half an hour. Peel the pears, cut them into pieces and cook them in a ladleful of water plus half a small glass of Calvados, a good grinding of pepper, the cloves, grated rind of half an orange and the cane sugar.

Use a fork to mash the cooked pears into a puree, and dry them off over a high heat. Put the ball of pastry dough between two sheets of oven paper and use a rolling pin to roll it out very thinly. Line 4 little tartlet tins, each 10 cm in diameter, with oven paper, cover this with pastry and prick the base with a fork. Put aluminium foil on top of the pastry, and then put in dried beans to prevent the pastry rising in the middle. Bake the pastry cases blind for five minutes in the pre-heated oven at 200 C. (390 F.). Remove the pastry cases from the tins, spoon in the pear puree, cover with thin slices of apple, brush with melted butter and bake for a further 20 minutes at 200 C. (390 F.). Serve the tartlets with a dusting of icing sugar.

Bartolomeo Bimbi, *Plums,* Poggio a Caiano, Villa Medicea, Florentine galleries (in storage)

Petto di tacchino farcito alle prugne / Turkey breast with prune stuffing

900 g (2 pounds) turkey breast
½ an apple
½ a pear
60 g (2 oz) prunes
40 g (1 ½ oz) nut kernels
40 g (1 ½ oz) bacon
a small glass of brandy
20 g (1 oz) butter
½ glass dry white wine
rosemary, salt and pepper

Chop into little pieces the fresh fruit, the prunes and the nuts. Slice the bacon very thinly. Mix it all together and season with the brandy.

Make a cut in the turkey breast, lengthways so as to form a pocket, and fill this with the prepared fruit stuffing. Sew up the opening with a white thread.

Put the turkey meat in a baking dish together with the butter and rosemary. Season with salt and pepper, and cook in a hot oven, at 180 C. (350 F.) for about an hour and a quarter, moistening it from time to time with the white wine.

Tortino dolce di susine / Sweet plum pie

500 g (1 pound) "Regina Claudia" plums
butter
2 eggs
130 g (1 cup) flour
400 g (1 ½ cup) milk
2 tablespoons icing sugar

Chop the plums in half and remove stones, then arrange the plums close together in a well-greased pie dish.

Beat the whole eggs together with the sugar, flour and milk and pour the resulting batter on to the fruit. Place the pie in a pre-heated oven (180 C.) (350 F.) and cook for 40 minutes. Serve warm, sprinkled with icing sugar.

Giovanna Garzoni, *Plate with plums, jasmines and nut,* Florence, Pitti Palace, Palatine Gallery

Salsa di noci / Walnut sauce

500 g (1 pound) walnuts
½ garlic clove
extra virgin olive oil
bread without crust
cream, salt

Crack the nuts and put the kernels into boiling water for a few minutes so as to peel them more easily. Put a few kernels at a time into a mortar (preferably of marble or wood), or else into the blender, and add the bread previously softened in water and well squeezed, plus the garlic and the necessary salt. Pound (or process) the ingredients to make a smooth mixture. Put it into a bowl and dilute with a little cream mixed with three tablespoonfuls of oil.

Gnocchi con susine della Giovanna / Giovanna's little plum dumplings

For the dumplings:
1 kg (2 pounds) floury potatoes
250 g (2 cups) flour
1 egg
nut-sized piece of butter
salt

For the dressing:
100 g (4 oz) butter
2 tablespoons very finely grated breadcrumbs
2 tablespoons sugar
1 tablespoon powdered cinnamon

For the filling:
20 ripe soft plums (the little dark violet kind of plum would be perfect)
25 g (1 oz) butter
2 tablespoons breadcrumbs
1 tablespoon sugar
1 teaspoon powdered cinnamon

Boil the potatoes in their skins, starting them off in cold water. Meanwhile, prepare the filling. Melt the butter in a small frying pan, add the breadcrumbs and brown them for a few minutes on a very low heat. Take them off the stove, add the sugar and cinnamon, and mix well. Wash the plums, remove the stalks, and make a small vertical cut in each plum to take out the stones, leaving the plums whole. Put a little bit of the filling inside the hole left by the stone, and close up the plums into their original shape.

When the potatoes are cooked, peel them whilst still warm, and pass them through a potato masher on to a floured pastry board. When they are tepid, add the beaten egg, butter and salt, and then the sieved flour, a little at a time. Mix it all into a dough and work it until it is smooth and all ingredients well blended together. Form the dough into a cylinder shape and cut off pieces the size of a small mandarin. Flatten these out to make discs about 1 cm thick. Put a stuffed plum in the centre of each disc and close it up like a little parcel. Seal it well and then roll the dumpling between floured hands to give it a round shape. Put a panful of water on the stove and when the water starts to boil, add salt, and put in the dumplings. When these float to the surface, take them out with a slotted spoon and arrange them on a serving dish.

Sprinkle them with a mixture of sugar and cinnamon. Melt the butter over a gentle heat, add the breadcrumbs, brown them briefly and then pour the very hot butter over the dumplings.

Anonymous Florentine Artist, *Fruit stands with fruit and vegetables,* Florence, Pitti Palace (in storage)

Pecorino e pere gratinate / Baked pears with sheep's cheese

300 g (10 oz) sheep's milk cheese
2 "Kaiser" pears
extra virgin olive oil
salt, pepper
honey

Pre-heat the oven to maximum. Peel the pears and cut them into thin slivers. Thinly slice the cheese, first removing the rind. Use the oil to grease four oven pans. Place into them first the slivers of pear, then of cheese, then a sprinkling of salt and pepper and a few drops of oil. Cook them in the pre-heated oven for a few minutes, then serve just as they are in the oven pan or tray, with a little chestnut honey added to each as a final touch.

Confettura di fichi acerbi / Green fig jam

500 g (1 pound) small unripe figs
1,200 g (2 ½ pounds) sugar
2 lemons
1 vanilla pod

The figs should be about the size of a walnut. First, clean them with a cloth, then prick them with a needle and place in a saucepan. Cover with cold water and bring to the boil. Strain, replenish with cold water and bring again to the boil. Repeat the operation at least five times, adding on the last boil a strip of lemon peel. Strain the figs as before and remove any remaining stalks. Chop the figs in half. Place the sugar in a large saucepan with a cupful of water and allow to dissolve, stirring well over a low heat. Add the vanilla and boil for 15 minutes until the syrup thickens. Take away the vanilla, add the figs and cook for a further 10 minutes, then add the juice of the two lemons, continuing the cooking for another 10 minutes.

Check consistency before proceeding to pot the jam.

Composta di ciliegie al vino / Compote of cherries in wine

600 g (1 ½ pounds) ripe black cherries
a glass and a half of red wine
3 heaped tablespoons of sugar
rind of half a lemon
1 clove
a small piece of cinnamon

Put the wine in a saucepan and add the sugar, the lemon rind cut into spirals (without the white pith), a small piece of cinnamon and the clove. Cover the pan, and bring the contents to the boil over a moderate heat. Wash and stone the cherries, and remove the stalks. Put the cherries into the saucepan, and cook them for five or six minutes over a moderate heat with the pan lid on. Take them out of the pan with a slotted spoon, and put them in a glass dessert bowl. Reduce by half the liquid in the pan, discard the lemon rind and spices, and pour the liquid over the cherries. Cover the

bowl with transparent cling foil and keep it in the fridge until ready to serve. This mixture can be poured over thin slices of sponge cake, transforming it into a "cherry soup", served in small individual dessert bowls garnished with a whipped cream.

Giovanna Garzoni, *Plate with cherries, broad bean and hornet,* Florence, Pitti Palace, Palatine Gallery

Torta di ciliegie / Cherry tart

For the pastry:
300 g (10 oz) flour
150 g (5 oz) butter
salt

For the filling:
800 g (2 pounds) stoned black
cherries
200 g (7 oz) sugar
1 tablespoon corn flour
150 g (5 oz) butter

To glaze the tart:
1 teaspoon icing sugar
2 tablespoons milk

Sieve the flour on to the pastry board, make a well, and in the middle put the softened butter, in little pieces, and a pinch of salt. Work the flour and butter together with the fingertips until the mixture has the consistency of large breadcrumbs. At this point add 6 or 7 tablespoons of cold water and work the ingredients together just enough to make a smooth dough. Form this into a ball, wrap it up in a clean cloth, and let it rest in the fridge for about an hour. Mix the sugar with the corn flour, and add it to the stoned cherries, together with the juice which came from the cherries when the stones were taken out. Stir it well together, and let the mixture rest for about 20 minutes.

Butter and flour a baking tin, 26 cm in diameter.

Divide the pastry into two, one piece double the size of the other and roll out two discs about 3 or 4 mm. thick.

Line the baking tin with the larger pastry circle, letting it overlap the sides of the tin. Spoon in the cherry mixture and cover this with the smaller pastry circle. Adjust the pastry round the edge of the tin, removing any excess and pinching it together so that both pieces are well joined.

With a small pointed knife, cut a little hole about 1 cm in diameter in the middle of the tart and insert a little cylinder of cardboard lined with aluminium foil to allow the steam to escape. Use any leftover bits of pastry to make decorations which can be stuck on to the top of the tart with a few drops of cold water. Dissolve the icing sugar in the milk, and brush this over the surface of the tart. Bake in the oven, pre-heated to 220 C. (420 F.) for 10 minutes, then reduce the temperature to 160 C. (320 F.) and continue cooking for a further 4 - 5 minutes. Serve the tart straight out of the tin, lukewarm, with whipped cream.

Tortino dolce di ciliegie / Sweet cherry tart

2 whole eggs
350 g (1 ½ cup) milk
130 g (1 cup) flour
50 g (2 oz) sugar
30 g (1 oz) melted butter
7-800 g (2 pounds) stoned
cherries

Beat the eggs together with the milk, flour, sugar and melted butter to make a smooth even liquid batter.

Pour the batter into a greased pie dish and distribute the stoned cherries on top. Cook the tart at 180 C. (350 F.) for about three quarters of an hour and serve while still warm.

Ciliegie in agro dolce / Sweet pickled cherries

500 g (1 pound) cherries
1 litre (4 cups) white vinegar
150 g (5 oz) sugar
5-6 cloves

Clipping short the stalks where necessary, place the cherries in wide-necked glass jars which can be hermetically sealed. Pour the white vinegar with the sugar and cloves into a saucepan, and boil for several minutes. After this pour it - still boiling - over the cherries, and close the jars.

Allow at least a month to go by before opening and using. These pickled cherries form an excellent accompaniment to boiled meat, to roast duck and roast meat in general.

Bartolomeo Bimbi, *Peaches and apricots*, Poggio a Caiano, Villa Medicea, Florentine galleries (in storage)

Petto di anatra alle pesche / Duck breast with peaches

2 duck breasts
2 yellow peaches
Calvados liqueur
meat stock, flour, butter
salt and pepper

Brown the duck breasts in butter on both sides.
Season the meat with salt and pepper, remove it from the pan, drain from the pan all the fat, and replace the meat. Sprinkle this with some Calvados liqueur, and allow it to evaporate. Now set the breasts to one side, but do not allow them to cool. Peel and stone the peaches, chop them into pieces and soften them for five minutes in the dripping from the meat. Remove the peaches, and thicken the fluid with a tablespoonful of flour and a little stock to make a gravy.
Cut the breasts into slices (the meat should still be pink in the middle). Cover with the gravy and garnish with the sliced peaches.

Dessert fresco di albicocche / Fresh apricot dessert

10 apricots
4 tablespoons cane sugar
1 lemon

Choose apricots which are just ripe. Wash and stone them, then place on a tray, with the hollow centres uppermost. Sprinkle with the juice of the lemon and the cane sugar. Refrigerate for at least three hours before serving.

Peschenoci alla griglia profumate all'amaretto / Grilled nectarines flavoured with amaretto liqueur

8 nectarines
1 vanilla pod
1 teaspoon cinnamon
2 tablespoons sugar
150 ml (½ cup) amaretto liqueur
(4 passion fruits, optional)
500 g (1 pound) mascarpone
(sweet cream cheese)

Pre-heat grill and oven to 190 C (370 F.) Chop and stone the nectarines. Place them under the grill with the fleshy part face down until they start to turn a golden colour. Mix the sugar with the cinnamon. Arrange the nectarines on an oven tray with the flesh uppermost. Sprinkle with the flavoured sugar. Pour the amaretto liqueur into the centre of the tray and cook the nectarines in the oven for ten to fifteen minutes until tender. Allow to cool and then serve with very fresh mascarpone and decorate, if desired, with the passion fruit.

Giovanna Garzoni, *Fruit stand of peach with fig and "bazzaruole"*, Florence, Uffizi Gallery,
Drawing and print cabinet

Pesche affogate della Giovanna / Giovanna's drowned peaches

800 g (2 pounds) ice cream
3 very firm yellow peaches
300 g (10 oz) sugar
1 vanilla pod

For the sauce:
200 g (7 oz) raspberries
100 g (3 ½ oz) sugar

Scald the peaches using plenty of boiling water - so that they are fully covered. Take them out after one minute and rinse them in cold water, then peel and halve them (the peaches should be of the sort where the stone comes away easily)
Boil 300 g (10 oz) of sugar with the vanilla in 3/4 litre of water until the sugar has dissolved, then add the peach halves, cover and reduce heat to its lowest setting. Simmer for four or five minutes. Now take the saucepan from the hob and let the peaches cool in the syrup.

Cook the sugar for the sauce and the raspberries together over a low heat for three or four minutes, mashing the raspberries to make a thin sauce. Just before serving divide the ice cream between six goblets, crushing it lightly, then add the six cold peach-halves drenched and dripping with syrup.
Pour the raspberry sauce on top and then serve.

Tortino dolce di pesche / Peaches in batter tart

1 kg (2 pounds) firm yellow peaches
120 g (1 cup) flour
4 eggs
100 g (3 ½ oz) sugar
½ litre (2 cups) milk
50 g (2 oz) butter (plus some for the pie dish)
a small glass of Cointreau
1 tablespoon of icing sugar
salt

Melt the butter in a "bain marie" in a small pan, and allow to cool. Break the eggs into a bowl, add the sugar and a pinch of salt and beat together for a few minutes with an electric whisk until the mixture starts to turn white. Add the milk and the sieved flour. Continue to whisk so that all ingredients are well mixed. Lastly add the liqueur and the melted butter so that the final mixture consists of a thin batter.

Grease a pie dish (pirex or porcelain, 26 cm in diameter).
Peel and quarter the peaches and arrange them in the pie dish. Pour over the batter and cook for about an hour in a pre-heated oven at 180 C. (350 F.) Take the batter out of the oven and use a small sieve to sprinkle icing sugar over it whilst still hot. Serve either cold or warm in the pie dish in which it was cooked.

Giovanna Garzoni, *Dish with medlar fruit, almonds and one rose,* Florence, Pitti Palace, Palatine Gallery

Mostarda di rosa canina / Wild rose hip "mostarda"

1 kg (2 pounds) fruit (rose hips)
500 g (1 pound) sugar
1/2 litre (2 cups) vinegar
cinnamon
cloves
orange peel

Cook the de-seeded rose hips in boiling water for a few minutes, then drain them, and whilst they are drying, prepare a syrup by boiling together the vinegar, sugar, cloves and cinnamon, plus the grated peel of one orange. Add the fruit and boil for a further five minutes.

Put the fruit into jars and cover it with the syrup.

Marmellata di coccole di rosa canina / Wild rose hip jam

2 kg (4 pounds) rose hips from wild roses
sugar
2 litres (8 cups) dry white wine
1 lemon
alcohol, 90°

Wash the rose hips, cut them in two and use a teaspoon to remove the down and pips. Put the fruit in a stainless steel pan, cover with wine and let it steep for a week, giving it a stir every day. (Cover the pan with a table napkin, and keep it somewhere in sight). At the end of the week, put the pan on a medium heat and cook the contents for 30 minutes, timed from the moment the fruit started boiling. Pass it through a fine-meshed sieve or vegetable mill. Weigh a pan, put in the rose hip puree, and calculate the net weight of the fruit by subtracting the weight of the empty pan from the sum total. Add an amount of sugar equal to the weight of the fruit, and the juice of one lemon for each kilo of weighed fruit. Bring it back to the boil, stirring frequently. Continue cooking until a teaspoonful of the mixture on a sloping plate stays set and firm. Fill it into warm, clean jars whilst still hot, and let it cool completely for at least 24 hours.

Place a disc of alcohol-soaked paper on top of the jam before sealing the jars hermetically. Store in a cool, dark and dry place.

Insalata alle mandorle / Almond salad

250 g (10 oz) mixed salad (green
and red lettuce, curled endive,
"lollo" salad)
150 g (5 oz) lightly toasted
almonds
3 tablespoons balsamic vinegar
2 tablespoons almond oil
2 tablespoons groundnut oil
1 dl (½ cup)) cream
1 tablespoon mustard
salt and pepper

Thoroughly wash and dry the different kinds of salad and place in a bowl with the chopped almonds. Pour the vinegar, the almond and groundnut oils, the cream, mustard, a pinch of salt and a grinding of pepper into a shaker, shake together for a few seconds, then pour the vinaigrette over the salad, mix well and serve.

Nucato / Nougat

1 kg (2 pounds) flower honey
1 kg (2 pounds) almonds
(walnuts or nut kernels)
1 lemon
Spices:
1 teaspoon powdered ginger
1 pinch of pepper
1 tablespoon powdered cinnamon
1/3 teaspoon powdered cloves
oven paper

Warm the honey over a gentle heat, skimming it well. Roughly grind the almonds (or other nuts). Combine with the honey and continue cooking, stirring continually. About 35-40 minutes' cooking over a low heat will be necessary, stirring all the while.

The nougat is ready when the almonds can be heard softly crackling under the heat. Do not let them turn brown as this will make the nougat bitter. The mixed spices are added in two stages: 1 teaspoon at the outset, and the rest towards the end. When the nougat is cooked, spread it while still boiling over a tray lined with oven paper and level it off with a spatula. Wait until it is completely cool before serving.

Giovanna Garzoni, *Melon and slice of vater melon,* Florence, Pitti Palace, Palatine Gallery

Risotto al melone / Melon risotto

600 g (1 ½ pound) frozen melon pulp
150 g (5 oz) icing sugar
1 egg white
a small half cup of Cointreau liqueur
Champagne (Spumante)

Peel the melon. Beat or mash half, the other half chop into cubes. Finely chop the shallot and brown it lightly in a saucepan with the butter and oil. Add the cubes of melon and allow them to absorb the flavour for a few minutes. Set some of the cubes to one side to use for garnishing the risotto. Now add the rice, let this take on the flavour, pour in the wine and let it evaporate. Then add the stock and let the rice cook. A few minutes before taking the rice off the stove, adjust the salt seasoning, and add the melon pulp and pepper. When the rice has finished cooking, let it rest for a few moments, then add the cream and a tablespoon of butter, mixing them in carefully. Serve garnished with strips of ham and the melon cubes set to one side.

Melone al porto / Melon flavoured with port

2 very ripe small melons
red port wine

Cut the ripe melons in two. Extract the seeds and filaments with a corer, forming a hollow. Fill the hollow with red port wine. Put the melons in the fridge until needed. Before bringing them to the table, empty them and pour in fresh port, since the old will have taken on a "watery" flavour. Serve with a dessert spoon suitable for scooping out and savouring the deliciously port-infused melon flesh.

Sorbetto di melone allo spumante / Melon sorbet in champagne

600 grammi di polpa di melone congelata
150 grammi di zucchero a velo
un albume
mezzo bicchierino di Cointreau

Whisk together the frozen melon pulp with the egg white, the sugar and the liqueur so as to obtain a quick sorbet. Put it in the freezer for a quarter of an hour and then serve each scoop of the sorbet drenched in ice-cold champagne.

Jan Fyt (?), *Still life with small monkey and puppy,* Florence, Pitti Palace, Palatine Gallery

Fichi caramellati / Caramelised figs

40 g (2 oz) sugar
8 ripe figs
1/2 a glass of Marsala

Dissolve the sugar in a spoonful of water in a saucepan over a moderate heat. When the sugar has just begun to turn gold and caramelised pour on the Marsala and turn off the heat. After a minute, when the wine has partially evaporated, add the figs and stir them in carefully so that they are evenly covered with the caramel. Serve with ice cream.

Fichi gratinati / Baked figs

1 kg (2 pounds) well-ripened figs
300 g (10 oz) castor sugar
whipped cream

Dopo averli lavati e asciugati, mettere i fichi ben maturi in una pirofila. Spolverizzare con abbondante zucchero e passarli al forno ben caldo lasciandoveli fino a che lo zucchero si sarà caramellato. Si servono freddi con panna montata.

Sorbetto di lamponi / Raspberry sorbet

500 g (1 pound) raspberries
250 g (1 cup) sugar
juice of half a lemon
half an egg white
4 mint leaves

Make half a litre of syrup by boiling 250 g (8 oz) of sugar in an equal amount of water. Let this cool completely and then blend in the raspberries, rubbing them through a sieve, plus the juice of half a lemon. Carefully fold in half a stiffly-beaten egg white, and then put the whole mixture in the ice cream machine.
Serve the sorbet in little glass goblets, decorated with a few leaves of mint.

Bartolomeo Bimbi, *Grapes,* Poggio a Caiano, Villa Medicea, Florentine galleries (in storage)

Schiacciata con l'uva / "Schiacciata" cake with grapes

1 kg (2 pounds) black grapes for wine, a small sweet variety
500 g (1 pound) bread dough
3 tablespoons extra virgin olive oil
1 sprig of rosemary
3 tablespoons sugar

This recipe dates from the time of the Etruscans, who used honey in place of sugar. Wash the grapes, dry them and remove the stalks.

Lightly fry the oil and rosemary on a very low heat, and after this, when completely cool, remove the rosemary and add the oil to the bread dough, working it in thoroughly for quite a while. When the oil has been completely absorbed, divide the dough into two equal parts, roll it out 1 cm thick, and place one half of dough in a greased baking tin. Cover thickly with grapes, and then put the second half of dough on top, pinching it all round so as to seal it well. Having pricked holes in the dough on top, sprinkle it with plenty of grapes and dust with sugar. Cook for 40 minutes at 180 C. (350 F.) in the oven (a wood-fired oven if possible). Let it cool completely before serving.

Sorbetto d'uva / Grape sorbet

500 g (1 pound) sweet white grapes, (well washed and de-seeded)
2 small glasses of grappa liqueur
2 tablespoons sugar

Steep together the grapes, the grappa and the sugar for at least eight hours. At the end of this time, rub it all through a sieve and put the thick juice obtained into the ice-cream machine and whisk it round. Leave it to set firmly in the freezer for about an hour before serving in little goblets.

Uva brinata / Frosted grapes

little bunches of sweet white grapes
1 egg white
castor sugar

Thoroughly wash and dry small bunches of sweet white grapes. Quickly dip them in the lightly beaten egg white, and sprinkle them generously with sugar, so as to coat them completely. Once the egg white has dried out, the grapes will have a lovely frosted appearance.

Strawberries, cherries, redcurrants and mandarine segments can all be frosted in a similar way.

Cerchia di Baccio del Bianco (?), *Fruit stands and hampers of fruit on shelves and wine in ice container,*
Poggio a Caiano, Villa Medicea, Florentine galleries (in storage)

Spiedini di frutta e verdure / Fruit and vegetables on little skewers

1 peach, 1 small melon
2 sticks of green celery
a small punnet of raspberries
12 strawberries, 1 green apple
2 slices of fresh pineapple
2 cucumbers, 6 small corn cobs
2 tablespoons of olives stuffed
with a tiny bit of vegetable pepper
1 green pepper
4 small tomatoes
cherries, grapefruit, black grapes
2 sticks of white celery
1 kiwi, 1 avocado, 1 small mango
4 palm shoots
12 whole blackberries

Take the peach, the melon, the green apple, green pepper, kiwi, avocado and mango, and cut them all into little chunks. Chop the green and white sticks of celery and the palm shoots into suitable small lengths, and use a small scoop to make little balls of cucumber. Halve the strawberries, the grapes and the stuffed olives. Cut the pineapple slices into small triangles, and the tomatoes into little segments.

Peel the grapefruit segments. The prepared fruit and vegetables can be arranged on little skewers for a spirited end to a summer meal.

Macedonia con frutta secca / Fruit salad with dried fruit and nuts

apples, pears, oranges, grapes,
mandarins, raisins, shelled
almonds
dried apricots
prunes, walnut kernels and figs
rum
sugar

Finely chop the various kinds of fresh fruit and sweeten with sugar. Cut the dried fruit and nuts into little pieces and soak them in rum for several hours, then drain, and add them dripping with rum, to the fresh fruit. Put the whole fruit salad in the fridge, and serve it cold and fresh, adding a few drops of orange flower water if desired.

Filippo Napolitano, *Refreshing bowl with fruit,* Florence, Pitti Palace (in storage)

Granita di Brachetto / "Brachetto" water ice

4 dl (2 cups) Brachetto wine
1 dl (½ cup) water
100 g (3 ½ oz) sugar
200 g (7 oz) strawberries

Put 80 g (2 ½ oz) of sugar in a saucepan, add the water, bring it to the boil and then let it simmer for 10 minutes. Turn off the heat and let it cool completely.

Put aside 2 tablespoonfuls of the Brachetto for the strawberries, then add the rest of the wine to the cold syrup, stir, and pour the mixture into ice-cube containers.

Put these into the freezer for four hours.

Wash and hull the strawberries, slice them thinly, put them into a bowl with the two tablespoons of wine previously set aside, and sprinkle them with sugar.

Let them steep, stirring them every now and then. Just before serving, break up the Brachetto ice cubes and serve together with the strawberries.

BERNAERTS Nicaise , known as MONSU' Nicasio (Antwerp, 1620-Paris, 1678)

A Flemish painter, a pupil of Frans Snyder, and a collaborator of Rubens and van Eyck, Monsù Nicasio owes his fame to his portrayals of still lifes and of animals.
After a stay in Italy and in France, he moved to Paris in 1663, where in collaboration with Charles Lebrun, he worked on preparatory designs for tapestry used in the manufacture of Gobelins. Four canvases of the artist are in the keeping of Florentine galleries, probably dating back to his stay in Italy. They are characterized by muted colour tones and delicate pictorial quality, well suited to the subtle collector's taste of Prince Ferdinando de' Medici, an expert judge of works of art.

BERTI Camillo, (Documented as being in Florence half-way through the 17th century)

Information concerning this painter is extremely scarce. He specialised in still lifes, and was close to the equally mysterious Giovanni Pini and "il Bigino".
The name Berti is cited in the inventory of pictures belonging to Don Lorenzo de' Medici in the Petraia villa in 1649. For the painting of The Poulterer, the artist's style, in various ways, came close to that of Chimenti (Jacopo da Empoli), Francesco Curradi and Cesare Dandini.

BIMBI Bartolomeo, (Settignano,1648 - Florence, 1723)

A pupil of Lorenzo Lippi and Onorio Marinari, Bartolomeo del Bimbo, known as Bimbi, devoted himself mainly to still life paintings, being attracted by the works of the Roman artist Mario de' Fiori, and of Agnolo Gori. He was one of the favourite artists at the court of the Medici. He decorated rooms, and produced pictures of flowers, fruit, shells and animals, also for a whole establishment for Prince Ferdinando and Cosimo III de' Medici.

CRESPI Giuseppe Maria, known as "The Spaniard" (Bologna, 1665-1747)

The artist owes his nickname of "The Spaniard" to the style of clothes he liked to wear. His artistic education was in Bologna beside Canuti, Cignani and Burrini. His travels in various parts of Italy remained a fundamental part of his experience, giving him the opportunity to deepen his knowledge of the works of Carracci, Guercino, Reni, the 16th century Venetians, and of Correggio, Barocci and Mattia Preti. He was attracted by common, popular subjects and scenes from everyday life, rendered in a spontaneous manner, with sympathetic involvement. The Bolognese painter was on friendly terms with Prince Ferdinando de' Medici. He stayed in Florence on several occasions, where he was able to study important core Dutch and Flemish artistic works from the Medici collections, where he left, and sent, numerous still life and genre paintings.

DEL BIANCO Baccio (Florence, 1604-1656)

A person of many and versatile talents, Baccio del Bianco is noted as a painter, architect, civil and military engineer, scene-painter and designer, costume designer, deviser of tapestry weaving and of furnishings, graphic designer caricaturist, and garden designer. Contrary to what happened with his prolific output in commercial graphic arts, which are more documented, the catalogue of his pictorial productions is nevertheless uncertain, owing to the scantiness of trustworthy works among which are the decorative pictures of Casa Buonarroti in Florence.

FARDELLA Giacomo (Palermo? Active in Florence during the second half of the 17th century)

Information concerning Fardella is scarce. It is presumed that the artist - of self-styled nobility - was born in Palermo around the fourth decade of the seventeenth century. The painter, whose work shows the influence of the style typical of the Napolitan area, must have reached Florence about 1680, a fact born out by a series of recorded payments for 12 paintings commissioned by Prince Ferdinando de' Medici. Among these there is a record of a still life with fish, a lost series of four circular pictures and the great artistic composition of "Fruit, vegetables, game and fish with figures".

FYT Jan (Antwerp, 1611-1661)

A follower of Frans Snyders, Fyt was one of the principal exponents of seventeenth century Flemish painting, favouring still lifes of game and hunting scenes, which he depicted with particular finesse of colouring. Documents record his presence in Venice, Rome, Naples and Florence. The artist stayed in the Tuscan city from 1636-1637, a fact attested to by records of payments for paintings commissioned by Prince Lorenzo de' Medici and his nephew Giovan Carlo.

GARZONI Giovanna (Ascoli Piceno, 1600 - Rome, 1670)

One of the most famous miniature painters of her time, Giovanna Garzoni knew how to combine the lesson of the great Nordic masters with a subtle and delicate touch, whereby attention to nature and technical virtuosity are wedded together with rare poetic sensitivity and wholly feminine grace. Even in the past, Garzoni's splendid parchment miniatures portraying vases of flowers, and compositions of fruit and vegetables, were the source of inspiration for recipe books. Garzoni was active in Florence for a long time, from 1642 to 1651, enriching the Medici collections with numerous works, including several of her celebrated masterpieces.

LIGOZZI Bartolomeo (Florence, 1631/39 - 1695)

Grandson of the more famous Jacopo, a renowned painter of "naturalia" , Bartolomeo Ligozzi followed the family tradition as a still life painter. His work was appreciated by Cardinal Carlo de' Medici, and also by Vittoria della Rovere and by the Grand Prince Ferdinando de' Medici. During his stay in Rome towards the end of the 1660's, he became familiar with the work of Mario of the Flowers, and was attracted by it. Ligozzi's art is characteristically the meeting point between naturalism with a Nordic imprint (already actually produced by his grandfather Jacopo), and the more dramatic and vibrant influence of late Baroque painting.

MIGNON Abraham (Frankfurt on Main, 1640-? 1679)

A typical representative of Dutch still life painting, Mignon was an excellent artist, in the wake of Jan Davids de Heem. One of his celebrated compositions, in the keeping of the Uffizi, namely "Fruit and objects on the floor of a cabinet", reveals a pronounced technical virtuosity and a melancholy sense of the fleetingness of things, and of beauty.

MUNARI Cristoforo (Reggio Emilia, 1667 - Pisa, 1720)

Dedicated to the still life genre, in addition to the artistic culture of seventeenth century Italy, Munari was influenced by the analytical compositions of the Dutch school (such as those of Jan Davids de Heem), or by the German Christian Berentz, his friend in Rome (where he stayed from 1703 -1706). Having come into contact with Prince Ferdinando de' Medici, he remained in Florence for about a decade, from 1706. In Florence, he was also sponsored by Francesco Maria de' Medici and the Grand Duke Cosimo III. Among his compositions can be found still lifes, displays of precious objects and musical instruments, sometimes close to those of Evaristo Baschenis, and characteristic works of trompe-l'oeil, featuring sheets with drawings and engravings, quills and diverse objects.

NAPOLITANO Filippo (Naples?, 1587 - Rome, 1629)

After his artistic education in Naples, the artist moved to Rome as a protégé of Cardinal Francesco Maria Del Monte. In 1617 he moved on to Florence at the request of the Medici, where he remained until the death of Cosimo II in 1621. Above all, he is noted as a painter of landscapes, hunting scenes and battles. The painter is exceptionally represented in the Medici collections by several of his rare still lifes, which are characterized by a clear naturalism, in sensitive response to the teaching of Caravaggio, as shown by the three small canvases featuring "Two shells" "Two cedars" and "Bowl with fruit".

NAVARRA Pietro

Pascoli names Pietro Navarra as a pupil of Franz Werner von Tamm during that artist's sojourn in Rome, between 1685 and 1695. Some years ago he was identified as the artist kown as "Monogramist P.N.", a painter close to Spadino and Christian Berentz, whose monogram appears, for example, in the lower left on the volute of the capital included in a still life of the Galleria Nazionale d'Arte Antica, in Rome.

NUZZI Mario, known as Mario dei Fiori *(Mario of the Flowers)* **(Rome, 1603-1673)**

Mario Nuzzi known as Mario of the Flowers, was one of the most celebrated and imitated painters of flowers and still lifes in his own time. His paintings reveal a liking for decorative Baroque, combined with the influence of Flemish naturalism. Ancient documents listing the works of Mario de' Fiori in the Medici collections, record, among other pieces, a precious painted mirror, commissioned by Cardinal Giovan Carlo de' Medici, after much solicitation, in about 1648.

PINI Giovanni (Documented as being in Florence between 1633 and 1635)

There is no exact information on this painter of still lifes whose name appears in the 1649 inventory of the villa Petraia, and in other documents concerning the pictures belonging to Don Lorenzo de' Medici. They record the payment of the two paintings "with meat and salami" and "with fruit". The artist contends with the equally unknown Camillo Berti for the authorship of "Poulterer" and "Young man outside with food basket", respectively in the keeping of the Corridoio Vasariano and the Palazzo Pitti.

RECCO Giuseppe (Naples, 1634 - Alicante, 1695)

This artist followed the family artistic vocation, becoming the most important painter of still life in Naples. He was probably the son of Guglielmo (and not of Giacomo, as he had long been considered). He surpassed the Flemish style of the latter, afterwards being inspired by his uncle, Giovan Battista. He enriched his own figurative culture, with its neo-Caravaggesque imprint, during the course of a probable journey in Lombardy, which enabled him to study and become familiar with the work of Evaristo Baschenis, which seems to be demonstrated by the portrayal of elegant objects where flowers accompany plates of sweetmeats and musical instruments. His celebrated subjects of fish, shellfish, shells and fruit unite exquisitely bright colouring, the use of light and shade and skilled arrangement and spacing of shapes.

TANARI Antonio (Documented as being in Rome from 1604 - 1635)

At the end of the second decade of the 17th century, the Medici collection was enriched by the addition of still lifes, either painted in Florence, or originating from the Roman market, in accordance with the shared taste of Grand Duke Cosimo and his brother Carlo. This is the case with the two "Pictures of fruit", destined to adorn the Careggi villa of Cardinal Carlo de' Medici, carried out by the Roman painter and specialist of the genre, Antonio Tanari, and it also applies to the painting of "Fish", sent to Cosimo II in 1619, in which Tanari showed accuracy in naturalistic detail, probably deduced from treatises on the study of fish.

VALENTINO Domenico Giovanni (Rome?, active in Imola in the second half of the 17th century)

There is little information available on this painter, long referred to as "Master GDV" by the critics because of the initials placed on his canvases. A series of pictures portraying kitchen interiors, attributed to the artist, emphasises the picturesque aspects of ordinary people's lives, featuring furnishings and receptacles of various shapes and sizes, spread out in cheerful disorder. This is the case with "Kitchen Interior" in the Palazzo Pitti collection, which awakens interest in everyday life in the sane way as the themes of the Emiliano-Romagnolan culture which show a sympathetic awareness of common life and whose top exponent was the Bolognese Giuseppe Maria Crespi, a protégé and artist particularly liked by Prince Ferdinando de' Medici.

VAN AELST Willem (Delft around 1626/27 - still active in 1683, Amsterdam?)

One of the major exponents of seventeenth century Dutch pictorial art, Van Aelst owes his fame to the elegantly clear brilliance of his still life paintings. He stayed in Italy from 1649-56, mainly in Florence (from 1657 he settled in Amsterdam). His favourite theme was that of birds and game, portrayed with descriptive precision, an inclination for trompe-l'oeil, and radiantly rich colours. He also painted still lifes of flowers, fruit and crockery, in a manner approaching that of Willem Kalf. Cardinal Giovan Carlo de' Medici was the major patron of the Dutch painter, and in Cardinal Leopoldo de' Medici he found another important client .

VAN HOUBRAKEN Nicola (Messina, 1668 – 1720)

Sometimes mentioned under the name of Van Bubrachen or Van-de-Brachen, the artist was born in Messina into a family of Dutch painters. He moved to Tuscany at an early age and remained there until her death, producing still lifes of vegetables. Van Houbraken's painting, richly reminiscent of the North, but updated in taste and design, was appreciated by contemporaries, and by the Grand Prince Ferdinando de' Medici, who had a collection of "small formats" assembled in the Poggio a Caiano Villa, where he also included one of the artist's canvases depicting lettuces, artichokes and radishes.

VAN KESSEL, Jan (Antwerp, 1626-1679)

Van Kessel was a Flemish painter, a nephew and pupil of Jan Brueghel II, and also a pupil of David Teniers the Younger who inspired his pictorial style. His work stands out for its extreme skill and subtlety. Dedicated to still life painting, to scenes depicting animals and subjects of this kind, Van Kessel favoured small formats, mostly painted on copper.

Index

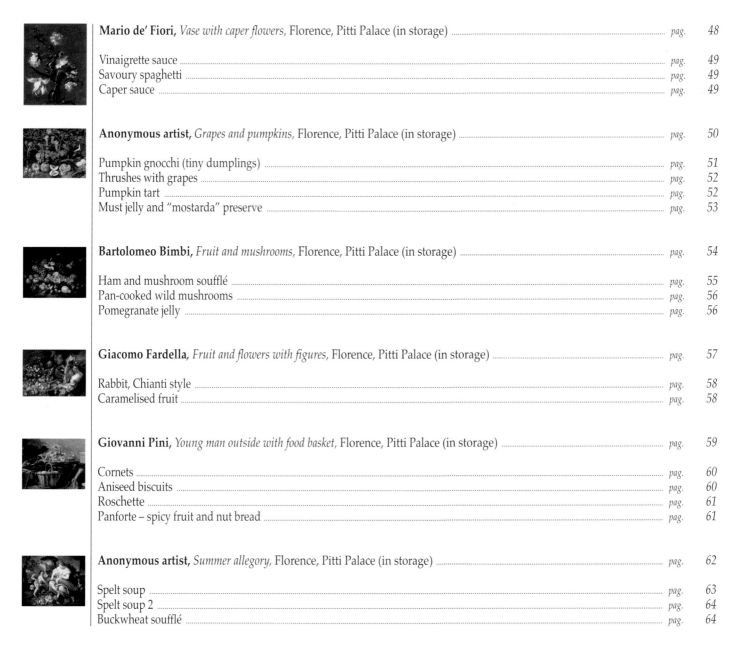

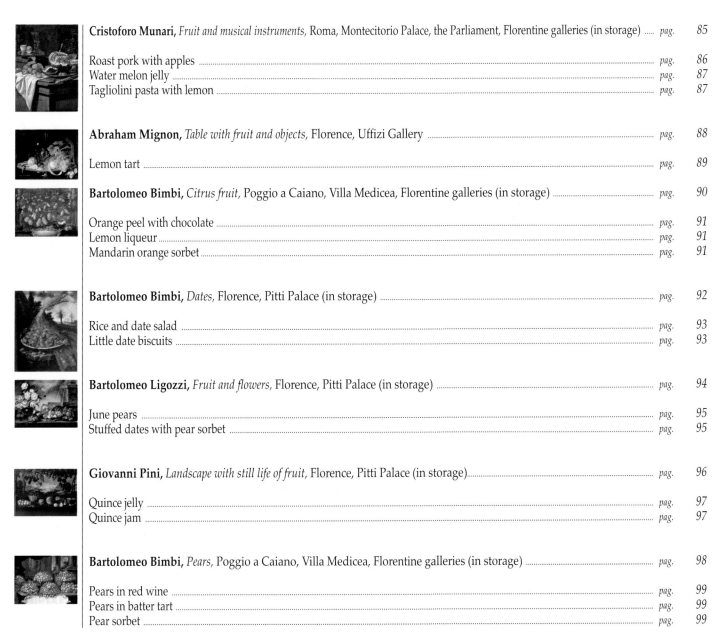

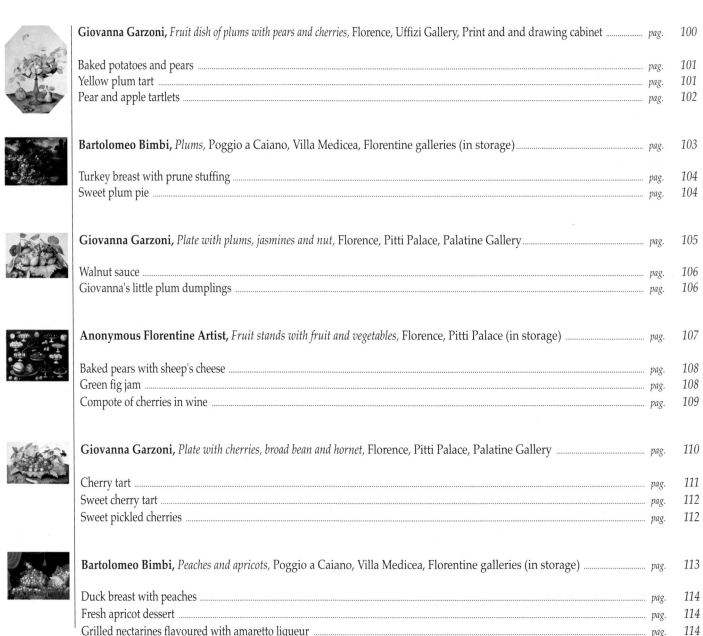

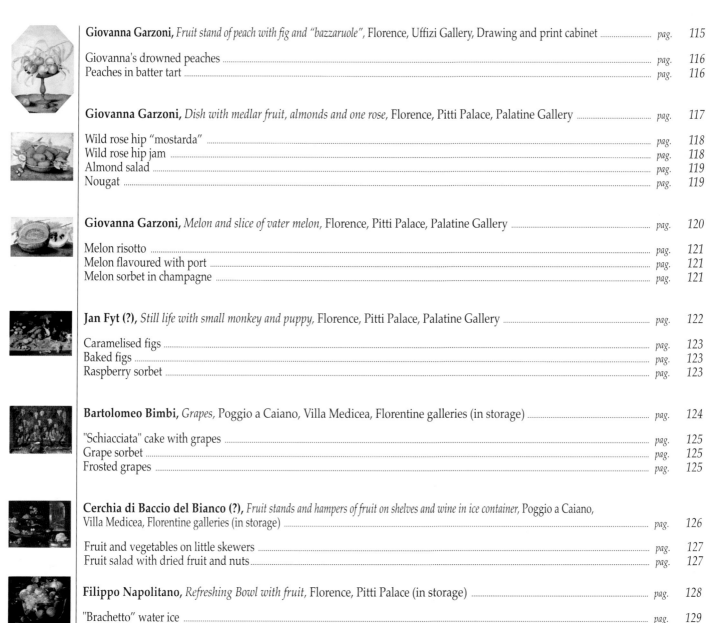

Analytic recipe index

finito di stampare
nel mese di novembre 2001
dalla tipografia: menegazzo/lucca
per conto di

maria pacini fazzi editore